EVERY MEMBER MATTERS

Why Your Church Needs You
and Why You Need Your Church

EVERY MEMBER MATTERS

Josh Wredberg
and Matthew Z. Capps

B&H
PUBLISHING®
BRENTWOOD, TENNESSEE

Printed in the United States of America

979-8-3845-1863-1

Published by B&H Publishing Group
Brentwood, Tennessee

Dewey Decimal Classification: 254.5
Subject Heading: CHURCH MEMBERSHIP /
CHURCH / MINISTRY

Cover design and illustration by Darren Welch Design.
Author photos by Maria Estes.

1 2 3 4 5 • 28 27 26 25

This book is dedicated to our church families, Fairview and Redeemer, whom we love deeply. Because of you, membership isn't a duty but a delight. It is our great joy to serve as your pastors.

I give thanks to my God for every remembrance of you, always praying with joy for all of you in my every prayer, because of your partnership in the gospel from the first day until now.

Philippians 1:3–5

Contents

Introduction

Pastor Will was walking through the parking lot after a Lord's Day gathering when a car pulled up beside him. The window rolled down, and Hellen introduced herself, "Hi, Pastor, it's so nice to finally meet you! I've been a member of the church for twenty-seven years."

Will had only been at the church for a few months but asked, "Why haven't we met yet?"

"Well, I haven't attended a church service in several years," she responded.

After they exchanged a few pleasantries, the pastor continued to his car, wondering how Hellen could consider herself a member of the church. After all, she wasn't involved in the life of the church at all. As Pastor Will talked to others in the church over the next few months, he realized very few people had a clear idea of what church membership called for. Unfortunately, this is far too common in the church today.

Between the two of us, we have too many memberships. Big box retail stores, online shopping services, the gym, alumni association, homeowner's association, the local pool, and of course, the church. Most of these memberships are similar. They affect only a small slice of life and demand nothing more than a minimal financial commitment and occasional attendance at an event. That's it. Nothing more.

Take, for instance, a membership at the gym. What are the expectations? Do you have to visit the gym a certain number of times in order to keep your membership intact? Are you kicked out of the gym if you fail to show up for a month? Is anything expected of you other than making sure your payment goes through? No, in fact most gyms are thrilled when members pay but don't show up. Your absence means less wear and tear on the facilities. The best kind of gym member is the one who pays but doesn't come.

Most memberships have a limited life cycle. If you keep making the monthly payment to the gym, you can keep your membership for as long as you want. But most people will eventually end the membership in order to save a few dollars. Some people move their gym membership regularly, as soon as a new one opens in their community with newer equipment and trendier decor. Rare is the person who keeps the same gym membership for a decade, much less for a lifetime.

Plus, the benefits of gym membership only affect a few aspects of your life. In the grand scheme of things, a gym membership will not provide the tools you need to have deeper friendships or a healthy marriage. No one goes to the gym for instruction on morals, work ethic, financial stewardship, or motivations for good deeds. While regular visits to the gym may help you experience a better quality of physical life, it has little implication on your soul.

Finally, no higher authority commands you to join a gym. Maybe your spouse makes a subtle suggestion about how a gym might help you get in shape or your company offers a health incentive for working out, but no authority figure demands that you join a gym. You are free to join, free to quit, and free to go back and forth. No command compels you to join your local health club.

Membership in the local church has little in common with other types of memberships. If you're a Christian, then you have been commanded to join a local church, and membership in that church positively affects every area of your life.

To make sure we are all on the same page, it might be helpful here to define what a church is. In the Christian tradition, the word *church* has been used two ways. First, the Church (uppercase) refers to all Christians across the world and time.[1] Second, the church (lowercase) refers to Christians who reside in a particular place to gather together regularly.[2] We often say the church (lowercase) is a local expression of the Church (capitalized). In this book we are primarily addressing the local church. In a local church, believers are bound together in commitment to one another to gather regularly and, among other things, receive faithful Bible instruction under recognized leadership and practice the ordinances (baptism and the Lord's Supper).

As you'll see in the first chapter, membership is not optional for the follower of Jesus. Church membership was practiced by the first Christians and is demanded for all following generations. The Bible lays out an expectation that every Christian would join a local assembly of Christians and be numbered with them.

And membership in the local church never has an expiration date; it's the only membership that doesn't end when you die. Your membership in the local, temporary assembly pictures your membership in the heavenly, eternal assembly. Death doesn't end your membership in the church. It simply transfers it to the final assembly.

Most of this little book explores how membership in the church differs from the other organizations you've joined because it demands something more than a monthly payment. Membership in the church demands all of you, and it impacts every aspect of your life.

When you join a gym, you're a member of the gym. That's it. But when you join a church, you're not just a member. You're also a worshipper, minister, and servant. You're a disciple-maker, giver, intercessor, and ambassador. These seven roles define what it means to be a member of the church.

One of the mottos regularly used by the United States Marine Corps is "Every Marine is a rifleman." No matter what specialty a Marine is trained to perform—everything from driving trucks to analyzing intelligence, from military police to cyber warfare—every Marine has to qualify with a rifle. You can't become a Marine without becoming a rifleman. The one identity—Marine—encompasses many roles. By accepting the title of Marine, you also accept all the roles that are included in the title. The same is true for the title "church member." That one title includes many roles. To separate the title from the roles is to weaken what it means to join a church.

If you allow our culture to color your understanding of church membership, you will likely dilute it until it becomes biblically unrecognizable. But if your view of membership is shaped by the Bible, you will see a fuller, richer, and more beautiful picture than you might have imagined. Joining a church can multiply the impact of your life in unexpected ways and is the doorway to a deeper experience of God's mercy and a more tangible demonstration of His care.

The goal of this book is to briefly unpack the beauty of God's design for the church, and how membership unlocks other God-given, grace-filled roles. This book is written by two pastors who love the church, serve in the same community, but in slightly different contexts. One of us pastors an older established church and the other pastors a younger church that began by meeting in a middle school.

Both of us have seen the impact meaningful membership has on the health of a church and the maturity of a believer. We understand that's not the case for everyone. Some have experienced tremendous hurt from church leaders and members, and we wish that were not the case. The church should be a place of healing, not hurting. Every church is made up of broken people, and no church is perfect. But we are convinced that you will never experience what God has saved you to experience without committing to a local church, and we want you to understand the deep joy that comes from joining your life to a group of other kingdom-minded Christians.

We don't know how you came to pick up this book. It was likely given to you by a pastor or close friend who cares about you. We hope you'll see this book for what it's intended to be. It's not a way for churches to improve attendance or increase giving. It's an invitation to participate in the great work God is doing through His church. We want you to join a gospel-preaching, mercy-displaying, kingdom-expanding church. If you do, if you go all in, we are confident your life, and the lives of those around you, will never be the same.

Chapter One

Why Membership Matters

So those who accepted his message were baptized, and that day about three thousand people were added to them. They devoted themselves to the apostles' teaching, to the fellowship, to the breaking of bread, and to prayer. Everyone was filled with awe, and many wonders and signs were being performed through the apostles. Now all the believers were together and held all things in common. They sold their possessions and property and distributed the proceeds to all, as any had need. Every day they devoted themselves to meeting together in the temple, and broke bread from house to house. They ate their food with joyful and sincere hearts, praising God and enjoying the favor of all the people. Every day the Lord added to their number those who were being saved.

Acts 2:41–47

In the early days of America, during the time of the founding of the country, a debate over independence raged in the halls of the Continental Congress. This meeting of delegates from each of the thirteen American colonies debated for months how to handle the growing animosity between England and America.

The debate was heated from the beginning, but when fighting broke out around Boston, the debate grew even fiercer. The representatives from the New England colonies were trying to get the congress to declare independence and develop a continental army. They had seen the fighting. Their friends and neighbors had been shot and killed. Their towns were laid waste by the bombing. They were already in the middle of the conflict. The southern colonies that were further from the fighting weren't sure they wanted to get involved. They were more comfortable as spectators.

Eventually, they all realized that success would only come when all thirteen American colonies represented in the Continental Congress joined together. They couldn't win the war with some colonies watching from the sidelines. The only way they could push back the enemies' forces was for every single colony to move to the front lines.

Christians are in a war. The Bible calls us soldiers,[1] tells us to fight the good fight,[2] and warns us about the enemy of our souls who's looking to destroy us.[3] For us to move forward, everyone must fight. The stakes are too high for any Christian to sit and watch the battle as a spectator.

The goal of this book is to challenge you to greater levels of commitment and engagement in the mission of God. Our prayer is that you won't be content watching the action and cheering others on, but that you'll see the need to engage fully in the life of your local church.

When it comes to the mission of God in our world, we believe the first step for every Christian is to join a church. If you are already a member of a church, this chapter is a reminder of what it means to be a member. If you are not a member, we hope it challenges you to think about why you should commit. If you're not a Christian, this chapter will hopefully give you a better understanding of how Christians attempt to live and serve each other in the church. Here are six reasons every Christian should become a member of a gospel-preaching church.

Reason One: Membership Follows the Pattern of the New Testament

In the book of Acts, we find the record of the birth of the church. Jesus ascends to heaven in chapter 1, and the Holy Spirit descends to us in chapter 2. After a great sermon by the apostle Peter during which 3,000 people become Christians, the church is birthed. Notice the next step: "So those who accepted his message were baptized, and that day about three thousand people were added to them" (Acts 2:41).

After they believed in Jesus, they were baptized and added. Added to *what* is the question. They were added to the church. The converts were numbered, baptized, and added to the church. In Acts, baptism is the initiatory rite into the church. The first Christians made their commitment to and inclusion in the church public, and from that point forward were considered a part—a member—of the church in Jerusalem. This pattern continued as the early church grew, day after day the Lord continued to add "to their number those who were being saved" (Acts 2:47).

The importance of being recognized as a member of the church is also reflected in Acts chapter 6 when a dispute arose in the church concerning care for the widows. Apparently, certain widows who were part of the church were not receiving food, while other widows were. "In those days, as the disciples were increasing in number, there arose a complaint by the Hellenistic Jews against the Hebraic Jews that their widows were being overlooked in the daily distribution" (Acts 6:1).

These neglected widows were considered a part of the church. They weren't random widows in Jerusalem. They were Christian ladies who had made a public commitment to the church and needed help from their church. The disciples addressed this issue by creating a new position in the church (which would later be called *deacon*), and they instructed the church to choose these servants from among the membership.[4] Following the disciples' instructions, the church chose from among themselves seven men of good repute, full of the Spirit and of wisdom, who were appointed to the task of caring for the widows.

We could look at other examples in the book of Acts, but the pattern is consistent. The church knew who was a part of the church. They knew who belonged to the church. When a person professed Jesus Christ as their Savior and was baptized, they were publicly added to the church—that's church membership.

This pattern is also evident in the letters of the New Testament. If you are not paying close attention, you may miss it. Notice how the apostle Paul often begins his letters by saying "to the church in . . .", and then names a specific city. The authors of the New Testament always assumed that the local churches to whom they were writing had a clear understanding of who was a member of the church and who was not. When Paul wrote to believers in various cities, he was writing to the local assembly of Christians in that city.

This becomes painfully clear when the apostle Paul pens his first letter to the church in Corinth. We discover something terrible taking place in the Corinthian church. One of the members is living immorally with his stepmother. The apostle Paul commands the church to remove the man from membership.[5] This may sound harsh, but this man is removed from the church for the sake of God's reputation, for the sake of the church's health, and for the sake of this man's soul. Ultimately, his removal from the church was done in love to show the seriousness of his sinful lifestyle.

The good news is, between the writing of 1 and 2 Corinthians, it seems the man repents of his sin, discontinues the immoral relationship, and comes back to Christ and the church. In 2 Corinthians 2, the apostle Paul encourages the church to accept him back into membership. He then describes what took place earlier when the church voted to remove this man from membership, to discipline him out of the church. "This punishment by the majority is sufficient for that person" (v. 6).

What does he mean by "the majority"? The majority of whom? Members! Unless you have a specific recognized number of members, you can't determine a majority. Church membership is not a recent addition designed to bolster attendance records. From the very beginning the early church practiced membership.

Finally, in Colossians 4:5, Paul distinguishes between those in the church and outside by calling the Colossian believers to walk in wisdom toward outsiders. In Galatians 6:10, Paul tells the believers in the Galatian churches to do good to everyone, especially to those of the household of faith. Simply put, this could only have been done if they knew who was "in" and who was "out" of that local church's membership.

Reason Two: Membership Provides Accountability for Sin

You need to join a church so you can be kicked out if needed. We're serious. Just consider the example of the man from the Corinthian church. This man was living in sin. Through his actions, he was denying the faith. Because he was a member of the church, the church could kick him out. What happened when he was kicked out? Once removed from the church he realized the seriousness of his sin, turned from it, and came back to Jesus. Placing someone outside the church is a serious move that shows the severity of their sin, the danger of their unrepentance, which hopefully wakes them up to the danger of their plight and saves them from final judgment.

One of the great benefits of church membership is accountability. Jesus gave the church a process called church discipline. He said:

> "If your brother sins against you, go tell him his fault, between you and him alone. If he listens to you, you have won your brother. But if he won't listen, take one or two others with you, so that by the testimony of two or three witnesses every fact may be established. If he doesn't pay attention to them, tell the church. If he doesn't pay attention even to the church,

> let him be like a Gentile and a tax collector to you." (Matt. 18:15–17)

At first blush, church discipline sounds mean, even vindictive. Is the point of church discipline to get revenge? Absolutely not. The point of church discipline is to see a sinning Christian restored to a right relationship with Jesus and with His people. This process of church discipline is an act of kindness. There is—or should be—grace in this pattern, as long as the circle of discipline is kept as small as possible for as long as possible. But in the end, kicking someone out is an act of grace intended to open their eyes. The motive for church discipline is love, and the goal is repentance and restoration so the one entangled in sin will escape judgment on the last day. Every warning before the final judgment is an act of love.

Accountability is why some Christians don't want to join a church. They think they're fine on their own, and they don't want anyone to challenge them. Not joining the church means no one will ever confront them for their sin, no one will ever get in their business. To put it another way, they are so worried about someone meddling in their affairs, they forfeit the mutual encouragement that comes from commitment to a local church. No one will be watching over them! When a Christian becomes isolated from the church, it affords the evil one a great opportunity. No one will be there to help them see the sin that so easily deceives them.[6] No one will be there to share their burden.[7] Sin is deceptive. Each of us is in danger of being deceived. But God, in His grace, gives us the church to protect us from self-deception.

Church discipline is like a life jacket. When you step in a boat and put on the life jacket, you don't want to use it. You don't want to need your life jacket. You don't want to get wet. You don't want to almost drown. But if something happens and the boat capsizes, you'll be glad you have the jacket on. You never want to be disciplined, but if you ever need it, you'll be glad for it. It's what God may use to save you from drowning in sin. Church membership is putting the life jacket on. Have you put the life jacket on? You may think you'll never need it—that's the type of thinking that leads to drowning. Are you a member of a church? Could you be disciplined if sin starts to swallow you? You may think it will never happen to you. No one ever does.

Reason Three: Membership Gives Protection from False Teachers

In Acts 20, the apostle Paul instructs the elders[8] of the church in Ephesus, "Be on guard for yourselves and for all the flock of which the Holy Spirit has appointed you as overseers, to shepherd the church of God, which he purchased with his own blood. I know that after my departure savage wolves will come in among you, not sparing the flock. Men will rise up even from your own number and distort the truth to lure the disciples into following them" (Acts 20:28–30).

The elders are to pay careful attention to the flock. Who is part of the flock? Does showing up on Sunday make someone a part of the flock? What about guests? What about travelers? How long does a person have to come before the elders have to pay careful attention to them? There has to be a way to know who is part of the flock—that way is church membership.

The reason the pastors need to pay attention to the flock is because wolves will invade the flock for the purpose of hurting the sheep. You may not have much experience with sheep, but can you figure out where the sheep are safest? They are safest in the flock with the other sheep under the care of the shepherd.

Some sheep mistakenly believe they will be safest on their own because the wolves won't notice them. That kind of thinking is why sheep are considered stupid. Predators love solitary sheep. For a wolf, a lone sheep is the equivalent of making a reservation at Outback. A solitary sheep is helpless and defenseless. It has no weapons. It has no one to protect it. It's not fast or cunning. A lone sheep will soon be dead meat.

Join a church for your safety. Life outside the flock may seem liberating, but so does skydiving without a parachute. Both always end badly. Membership gives you protection from false teachers who would harm you.

Reason Four: Membership Demonstrates Commitment to the Body

A couple of years ago, the *Huffington Post* ran an article called, "A Generation of Men Unwilling to Commit." This is how the article begins: "It seems men today overwhelmingly refuse to commit to long term relationships with women. For the most part, you'll find that many women love relationships and commitments. They dream of their Channing Tatum or Prince Charming with whom they can reenact scenes from their favorite romantic comedy. It's a generation of eternal bachelors whether you like it or not."[9]

The author gives a number of reasons he thinks men are unwilling to commit—because the grass is always greener elsewhere, because new women can't match up to a childhood love, and because of money and ambition. This article could be written about many Christians and their relationship with their current church. Whether it's because of money, ambition, previous experiences, or greener grass, too many Christians are noncommittal church bachelors, willing to date for years, but never marry.

In the Bible, the church is described as a building, a family, and a body.[10] These metaphors demand commitment. How good is a brick that won't stay in place in a building? What do people think of the family member who never shows up at the family gathering? What use is an amputated body part?

Families are built on commitment. Buildings are constructed with parts nailed, glued, and cemented together and then anchored deep into the soil so they won't fall. A body is woven together with veins, nerves, muscles, and bones. In other words, the church is a place where lives are to be intertwined. The church is a place where people are deeply committed to one another. As the apostle Paul says, "speaking the truth in love, let us grow in every way into him who is the head—Christ. From him the whole body, fitted and knit together by every supporting ligament, promotes the growth of the body for building itself up in love by the proper working of each individual part" (Eph. 4:15–16). God has woven members together into a body, and the body is to be growing together. This type of growth demands commitment. This metaphor doesn't allow for loose attachment. You definitely know what is part of your body. You know who is part of your family. You know what is part of your house. Membership allows everyone to know who is part of a particular church family, who is part of a certain house, who is part of a specific body. Membership allows everyone to know who is committed to growing together, and whose lives will be intertwined.

Reason Five: Membership Provides Clarity of Leadership

Imagine sitting at a local coffee shop during a work break, nursing an overpriced espresso, and your supervisor walks in and says, "Something has happened, and we need you at the office to help." Or your supervisor says, "You've been on break for way too long, we need you to get back to work!" How would you respond? Hopefully, you would jump to your feet and obey their request. They need your help, and you need to get back to work in order to keep your job. Imagine the same scenario with one different detail. The supervisor who walked into the coffee shop is not your employer. Would you respond the same way? No, you would not.

The writer of Hebrews exhorts the church: "Obey your leaders and submit to them, since they keep watch over your souls as those who will give an account, so that they can do this with joy and not with grief, for that would be unprofitable for you" (Heb. 13:17). Who are the leaders watching over your soul? You are commanded to observe their teaching and submit to their leadership in the church. Can any local pastor of any local church expect you to listen to him? Are you commanded to follow his leadership? God has given the church a leadership structure for a specific reason. The leaders need to know who is part of the church, and who's not. And church members need to know whose instruction to observe and whose to ignore. Membership provides clarity for you because it identifies who your leaders are, who has been called to watch over your soul. This is for your good!

Membership also provides clarity for the leaders of the church. Church leaders want to know for whom they will give an account. This verse weighs heavy on faithful pastors. Someday, we will stand and give an account for the people under our charge. We will stand before the God of heaven and give an account for the members of the church we pastor. This truth causes sleepless nights in pastors' homes. This truth should also remind pastors of the accountability they have before God concerning how they lead the church they have been called to serve. Membership shows pastors what sheep they are to watch out for, what sheep to count, what sheep to feed, and what sheep the owner will hold them accountable for when the day ends.

Reason Six: Membership Multiplies the Impact of Your Life

Before going up to the viewing area at the top of the Arch in St. Louis, you can watch a movie about how the arch was made. As the movie ends, the narrator says something profound. He says the arch is more than the sum of its parts. The final structure transforms everyday materials into something majestic. And he's right. Pieces of metal, concrete, steel—everyday materials—when joined together turn into something majestic.

That's how God designed the church. A bunch of everyday people—just sinners who've been forgiven by God—when joined together turn into something majestic. Through the church "God's multi-faceted wisdom may now be made known through the church to the rulers and authorities in the heavens" (Eph. 3:10). God is doing something majestic through a collection of everyday materials. God is taking a bunch of foolish rebels and displaying His wisdom to the watching powers.

We are everyday people—spouses, parents, students, employees, sons, and daughters. Our lives are short and most of us won't make it into a history book. Do you want to make a difference? Join your life to other ordinary lives and watch God do something extraordinary. Invest your life in something bigger than yourself. The church displays the wisdom of God to the cosmic powers. The church pushes back the gates of hell. The church heals the broken and hurting. And one day the church will marry Creation's King.

The church is the most broken and beautiful, despised and beloved institution in the world. Kingdoms will fall. Nations will crumble. Families will die out, but the church of Jesus Christ will last forever.

Conclusion

Are you a spectator or a participant? Are you on the sidelines or the front lines? It's easy to make excuses. "I'm too busy." "I'm too weak." "I'm too young." "I'm too old." How easy it would have been for those delegates of the Continental Congress to make excuses. "It's too risky, I'll lose everything. It's not my fight." But we know the story. We know how they staked their homes, their reputations, their very lives on the success of the American experiment.

You may be tempted to think you're too young to really engage in the church's mission. You're still a student, you still live at home, you're not a spouse or a parent. Did you know that more than a dozen signers of the Declaration of Independence were under the age of thirty-five? A number of the chief architects of America were in their early twenties during the Revolution, and some were still teenagers. You are not too young to make a difference. God can use your excitement and energy to do great things in your church and community. Don't wait until you're older to get involved.

Maybe you are on the other side, and you think you're too old to really make an impact. Your time is past, and all you can do is sit and watch. Samuel Whittemore fought in the Revolutionary War at the age of seventy-eight. He was in his fields when he spotted an approaching British brigade. He loaded his musket and ambushed the British. Whittemore was shot, bayoneted six times, and left for dead in his attempts to fight off the British army. When he was eventually found alive, the doctor said he would not survive his injuries. However, Whittemore lived another eighteen years until dying of natural causes at the age of ninety-six.

Age is no excuse—you may not be able to serve in the same way at eighty that you served at eighteen, but that's no reason to become a spectator. Make your life count for more. Join the church, where God takes the ordinary and does something extraordinary.

Chapter Two

Every Member a Worshipper

Let the word of Christ dwell richly among you,
in all wisdom teaching and admonishing one
another through psalms, hymns, and spiritual songs,
singing to God with gratitude in your hearts.
Colossians 3:16

Imagine you're at a friend's party one night, where you're introduced to a man in his late twenties. Let's call him Rico. You ask him what he does, and he says, "I'm a quarterback."

As a football fan, you're immediately interested and begin to ask him questions. "Really," you say. "Who do you play for?"

"Oh, I'm not on a team," he responds.

"Well, who did you play for in college?"

Again, Rico answers, "I didn't play on my college team."

"How about high school?"

"No, I didn't play on my high school team."

At this point, you're a little puzzled and ask, "So, what team do you or did you play quarterback for?"

"I've played quarterback my whole life, but I've never been on a football team. Teams are full of hypocrites. I don't need a team to play."

"Help me understand. If you're not on a team, how do you play quarterback, Rico?" you ask.

"While they're at the stadium playing games, I usually go out in the woods by myself and throw the football through a tire swing. It clears my mind. I feel like I'm connecting to the essence of football. It's more authentic than those quarterbacks who play on teams."

The quarterback in this story sounds delusional, doesn't he? After all, a self-proclaimed quarterback who never joins a team and only plays alone isn't really a quarterback at all, is he? The lone woodsman claiming to be a quarterback makes about as much sense as a Christian who never attends a church service but only worships alone.

Now, you may be thinking, *Worship is much broader than gathering with God's people on Sunday*. In one sense, that's true. All of life should be lived in worshipful response to God's goodness and grace. The apostle Paul urges believers to offer their whole life to God as spiritual worship[1] and to do everything including eating and drinking for God's glory.[2] However, Scripture holds forth a clear expectation for all Christians: God expects His people to worship with His people.

When we say that "every member is a worshipper," we mean that every Christian should be committed to attending the weekly gathering in order to listen to the Word of Christ with one another, sing with gratitude together, and then walk in wisdom alongside their fellow church members. This is the pattern of the first Christians, who gathered regularly for worship.[3] A holistic life of Christian worship is only possible within a local church because the church is not "simply a bunch of individual worshippers who happen to be in the same place and time. Individual worship is a subset that flows out of corporate worship."[4] You can't offer all of your life to God as worship if you refuse to offer Him Sunday morning to worship with the church.

Worshipping Against the Grain of Culture

We live in a culture where almost every experience is geared toward the personal pleasure and comfort of the individual. We are more fragmented than ever, and the church is not immune to this cultural wave. We have the power to cultivate a private set list of worship music on our devices, and we can select the type of preaching we want to hear by subscribing to our favorite preacher's podcast. Our concern is that many Christians have assumed that their spiritual journey is an individualistic affair. Not too different from the solitary quarterback in the woods.

The picture of corporate worship painted by Scripture does not reveal a service tailored to our own preferences and fulfilled at our own convenience. After all, the exhortation from the writer of Hebrews stands in stark contrast to our individualistic assumptions.

> And let us consider one another in order to provoke love and good works, not neglecting to gather together, as some are in the habit of doing, but encouraging each other, and all the more as you see the day approaching. (Heb. 10:24–25)

Look at the commands: Consider one another. Do not neglect to gather together. Encourage each other. How can these commands be obeyed outside of the regular gathering of a local church? Take 1 Corinthians 14:26 as another example, where Christians are reminded that when they gather, everything is to be done to build up one another. This simply cannot be accomplished outside of life within the local church.

So if all Christians should worship regularly in a local church, what should worship in a local church look like? As a church member, what role should you play in weekly worship? Well, there is a helpful three-fold pattern described in Colossians 3. In this pattern, we see that Christians are called to regularly gather with other Christians in order to receive the gospel, rehearse the gospel, and respond to the gospel in worship of Jesus.

Receiving the Gospel Together

Let's start by pointing out the obvious. You can't obey what Paul outlines in Colossians 3 if you don't show up to worship with other Christians. Unlike voting in an election with an absentee ballot, you cannot be a part of the worship gathering as an absentee member. Read Paul's words carefully.

> Let the word of Christ dwell richly among you, in all wisdom teaching and admonishing one another through psalms, hymns, and spiritual songs, singing to God with gratitude in your hearts. (Col. 3:16)

Do you see it? Paul says to let the word dwell richly "among you" and teach and admonish "one another." We receive the gospel together. The controlling command in this verse is to let the "word dwell richly."

A sponge helps us understand how we receive the gospel in the context of a church community. What happens when you squeeze a wet sponge? Whatever the sponge has soaked up comes out when it is squeezed. The goal of a church gathering is to soak one another in the gospel. We should saturate one another in teaching and admonishment. We should leave a church gathering drenched in gratitude. The reason is simple: When life's trials, tests, and temptations squeeze you, whatever you have soaked up comes out. The gospel should drip from you when you are wrung out like a sponge.

Colossians was written to a group of Christians who had gathered and established a church in the ancient Roman city of Colossae. The church was pastored by a man named Epaphras.[5] When they received this letter; they were to soak in it by reading and studying it in their weekly gathering.[6] This reminds us once again of the command to receive the Word in the context of a church community.

Before the invention of the printing press in the 1400s, studying the Bible in the context of a local church community was the only option for Christians. Many Christians today, especially in the West, have multiple copies of the Bible sitting on their bookshelf. This is a great personal benefit that the early church didn't have. Receiving the Word together was necessary for the early church, but modern Christians have begun to view it as one option among many. Perhaps we take for granted the blessing of communal Bible study the early church enjoyed out of need.

The church is the only gathering of people who have been given a book from God and have been gifted with the indwelling of His Spirit to understand and apply the book. We work out this blessing in the church community by "teaching and admonishing one another." Teaching means "to impart knowledge," and admonishing means "to correct behavior." Together they give the picture of a coach, not a professor. Someone who not only teaches another person but walks with them, showing them how to apply the truth to their situation.

Gospel-grounded churches are filled with life-on-life coaching. When the gospel fills us, we look for ways to pour it into other people's lives. Sometimes we use the gospel to encourage struggling Christians, and sometimes we use the gospel to confront sinning Christians—both in love and humility with the wisdom of Christ.

Whether encouraging or confronting, what we need is not our own thoughts but the thoughts of Jesus. And where do we find His thoughts? In His Word. People don't need our opinions. They don't need our perspective. They really don't need our suggestions. They need wisdom to handle the situation they're facing. God's Word equips us with the truth to share with others in times of uncertainty. Being present in the church's worship gathering, week after week, will shape the way you think to reflect the way Jesus thinks. A consistent diet of the gospel on Sundays prepares you to serve others throughout the week.

A missionary who served in Africa once said that he knew he had become fluent in another language when he began to dream in that language. Each Christian needs to learn a new language full of God's vocabulary, not their own. We must be so fluent in the gospel that even our dreams are biblical. As that happens, we can help each other in ways we never dreamed of.

Christian sanctification is as much a group project as it is an individual pursuit. In community study, we benefit from the insight, wisdom, and perspective of others. We hear from those at different life stages, enabling us to see through the rich prism of their experience. Christians need other Christians who speak God's Word to them. As J. I. Packer argues, "The church is to be a learning-and-teaching fellowship in which the passing on of what we learn becomes a regular part of the service we render to one another."[7] One clear benefit of receiving the Word together is that it allows us to rehearse the Word together.

Rehearsing the Gospel Together

The main purpose of Colossians is to teach Christians how to live together as those made alive by Jesus Christ. To live together in a way that honors Christ, we need to study and apply the Word of Christ together. Consider this instruction to the church:

> If you have been raised with Christ, seek the things above, where Christ is, seated at the right hand of God. Set your minds on things above, not on earthly things. (Col. 3:1–2)

These Christians have been raised with Jesus Christ. They are no longer dead in sin but are now alive in Christ. With this new life comes many questions about how to live. The apostle Paul tells them to live with their minds set on heavenly things. What does that look like? He spells it out by commanding them to "put off" certain worldly behaviors and activities like sexual sin, idolatry, anger, wrath, malice, slander, obscene talk, and lying.[8] That's a pretty comprehensive list, isn't it? Paul is telling them to discard sin like a dirty, stained, threadbare shirt. But the Christian life isn't just about saying "no" to sin. We also say "yes" to righteousness.

The next set of verses is full of commands to "put on" certain attitudes and activities.[9] The attitudes and actions Paul commands the church to "put on" can only be obeyed by participating in the local church. Take, for example, the command to "bear with one another."[10] You might think the easiest way to obey that command is to move to the wilderness and live in a cave. People can be difficult, so it's much easier to bear with others if you never have to see them or spend time with them. But God is not honored when Christians avoid those who are difficult. God is honored when we submit our hearts to Him and treat difficult people and situations with patience. God made us alive with Christ, and the fruit of Christ in us is patience with others. To dig even further, we're also told to "forgive one another." This implies we live in close enough proximity to each other to cause tension. As C. S. Lewis famously said, "Everyone thinks forgiveness is a lovely idea, until they have something to forgive."[11] The tension that necessitates forgiveness only comes when living in a close community with others.

Perhaps you remember those "rock tumbler" machines popular among children years ago. It was a simple device. A child would gather a handful of jagged rocks, throw them in the tumbler, and turn it on. The rough edges were worn off as the rocks tumbled together. At the end of the process, he'd open the tumbler and find that the jagged rocks had become smooth stones.

Rehearsing the gospel in the context of a church family works a lot like a rock tumbler. It wears the rough edges off. When we demonstrate the kind of patience and forgiveness Scripture calls us to in our relationships with others in the church, we bring honor to God. We worship Him.

The one another's referenced in the New Testament are other Christians in the church, so this work is only possible in the church. We "put on" living in such proximity to others in the church that situations arise where we need God to work in us to "bear with one another" and "forgive each other." And when that happens, God's glory is seen in His grace at work in our difficult relationships. This is only possible through the work of the Holy Spirit through us as we practice putting on love so we can live in perfect harmony and letting the peace of Christ rule in our hearts to live as "one body," the church.[12]

Your participation in the church is a necessary part of God's sanctifying process for you and others. God wants to change you, and He uses the church to do it. As part of the church, God uses you to change others. "It is easily forgotten that the fellowship of Christian brethren is a gift of grace," Dietrich Bonhoeffer wrote in his book *Life Together*.[13] If you refuse to join a church or only participate half-heartedly in the church, you have short-circuited God's transforming work in your life. If you want to follow Jesus, it means putting off some things and putting on others. God commands you to put on life in the church. To say, "I worship God alone. I don't need the church," says, "God, I know what Your Word says, but I'm going to ignore what You say and do what I think is best." That makes as much sense as playing quarterback in the woods by yourself. It's not authentic, but absurd. Like jagged rocks thrown into the rock tumbler of community, the rough edges of our life are worn down as we rehearse the gospel together through study and application of the Word. We end up as beautiful, smooth stones reflecting the image of Jesus Christ.

Responding to the Gospel Together

Finally, Paul says that we are to teach and admonish one another "through psalms, hymns, and spiritual songs, singing to God with gratitude in your hearts" (Col. 3:16). Have you ever considered that in our culture, the local church is one of the few regular gatherings of people who sing together? We might gather around the piano with family during Christmas to sing carols. We might even sing "Take Me Out to the Ball Game" with fellow sports fans at the occasional baseball game. But these instances are seasonal or irregular at best. In a local church gathering, we sing together and sing for one another regularly.

When Christians discuss singing in church, the conversation often turns to preferences over musical style. Interestingly, nothing is said in Colossians 3 about musical style. In fact, nothing is said in the New Testament about musical style. Even the Old Testament is relatively silent. We tend to discuss the style of music when the Bible focuses on the content of the music and the communal activity of our singing. Our songs are our theology. It's vital we sing songs rich in biblical truth. And it's vital that we sing together. Singing in church was never meant to be a spectator sport. We're all participants in praising God with song.

Both of us have the privilege of pastoring churches that love to sing. And when we gather with our church families week after week, the sounds of God's precious saints wash over us as we stand on the front rows of our gathering space. While the church sings, we've both quieted down to listen. Sometimes the sound of our congregation singing can be quite moving. It's moving not because our members are polished individual singers, but because together, the congregation makes a beautiful choir. One of the most moving experiences of congregational singing is hearing the people around us proclaim God's goodness in song during the highs and lows of life. It's hearing Ron belt out "Come Thou Fount" while fighting cancer. It's Lisa joining in the chorus of "Great Is Thy Faithfulness" after receiving an answer to prayer. It's being encouraged when Adam sings "My hope is built on nothing less than Jesus's blood and righteousness" after losing his job.[14] It's seeing Vic and April holding hands while praising God together after a difficult marriage season. No one has this rich communal experience while listening to their playlist with headphones on!

We've come to realize that worship isn't just something we do; worship does something to us. Our worship has a vertical aspect as we lift our voices to God and a horizontal aspect as we sing for one another. We believe this is what Paul had in mind when he admonished the Ephesians (just like the Colossians) to "be filled by the Spirit: speaking to one another in psalms, hymns, and spiritual songs, singing and making music with your heart to the Lord, giving thanks always for everything to God the Father in the name of our Lord Jesus Christ" (Eph. 5:18–20).

When the church sings as a whole, we are "speaking to one another," which admonishes and encourages us in the faith. As we will say often in this book, the "one another's" of the Bible cannot be accomplished in isolation from the local church. A singing church affirms that we are one in Christ and that we believe what we are singing regardless of where we are spiritually or emotionally as individuals. We need this encouragement from one another.

Conclusion

Chris and Justine were still reeling from the news they learned at the doctor's office on Friday. Two months ago, they were surprised to learn they were expecting their fifth child, and it didn't take long for their surprise to turn to joy. They couldn't wait to meet their little one. Because of Justine's age, the doctor had recommended genetic testing just to make sure everything looked fine. When the doctor called late Thursday afternoon and asked them to meet him in the morning to discuss the results, his tone of voice betrayed his concern. They entered his office holding hands and trying to force a smile. They sat down nervously and waited for the doctor to speak. The news was even worse than they feared. Though their baby's heart was beating fine and he was growing at a normal rate, the test revealed an irreversible medical condition that meant he could not survive outside the womb. They were devastated. After calling their family and pastor on the way home, the rest of the day and the next one blurred into one long period of mourning.

Sunday dawned sunny and beautiful. The weather felt inappropriate for the news that had shattered their world. They hadn't planned to go to church. It was all too much. But without even speaking about it, they both started to get ready. They glanced at each other, nodded, and continued their normal

Sunday morning routine. As they pulled into a parking space in the church lot, they took a deep breath and got out of the car. They found each other's hands and braced themselves for the onslaught of hugs and tears they knew was waiting for them. The next two hours were a blur. By the time they got back in the car, they were emotionally spent. Was it worth going to church that morning? Did it make any difference that they were in attendance?

Chris and Justine might not remember what was said that morning, but the people sitting near them vividly remember watching Chris and Justine worship in the midst of tremendous suffering. The faith of the middle-aged couple two rows behind them praying desperately for their wandering child was strengthened watching Christine sing through her tears. The widow to their right thanked the Lord for decades of joyful marriage because of the way Chris tenderly put his arm around Justine during the pastoral prayer. The most powerful preaching of the gospel that Sunday morning did not come from the pulpit but from the pew. Because Chris and Justine chose to worship together with the church, they were reminded of the gospel, and in their response they passed the gospel on to others. You can read the gospel by yourself, but when you worship as part of the church, you proclaim the gospel through your participation.

Chapter Three

Every Member a Minister

And he himself gave some to be apostles, some prophets, some evangelists, some pastors and teachers, to equip the saints for the work of ministry, to build up the body of Christ, until we all reach unity in the faith and in the knowledge of God's Son, growing into maturity with a stature measured by Christ's fullness. Then we will no longer be little children, tossed by the waves and blown around by every wind of teaching, by human cunning with cleverness in the techniques of deceit. But speaking the truth in love, let us grow in every way into him who is the head—Christ. From him the whole body, fitted and knit together by every supporting ligament, promotes the growth of the body for building itself up in love by the proper working of each individual part.

Ephesians 4:11–16

Many of our favorite stories and legends focus on a lone warrior who stands against a larger enemy, like General Maximus in a gladiator fight in the Roman Colosseum or Rocky Balboa in a boxing ring in Moscow. We celebrate underdogs who overcome all the odds to win the big game. The singular hero appears in our sports, books, and movies. It's no fun to cheer for the larger army to defeat the small one. We want a massive force of evil to be stopped by the heroic acts of a lone brave soldier. We like to think we can do it on our own. We don't need anyone else. All that's needed to win is our best effort.

This same thinking has crept into the church. All that's needed is Jesus and me. All that's necessary for my spiritual growth is my Bible and silence. The old hymn has become the current practice of many Christians: "I come to the garden alone . . . and He walks with me and He talks with me."[1] This popular version of Christianity masks a toxic strand of individualism, and church membership is one way to inoculate ourselves against this lethal virus.

Jesus has not called you to attempt the Christian journey as a solitary pilgrim. You cannot function faithfully as a Christian apart from significant participation in the church. You need others, and others need you. Following Christ requires connecting and contributing to His body, the church. The New Testament knows nothing of churchless Christianity. Perhaps you have heard it said, "You can't love Jesus and hate His bride." To be in Christ means we are in community with others who are in Christ. We are called to live out our Christianity within the context of the church.

But it's one thing to understand we need to participate in the church community, and it's another thing to understand what it looks like to be an active, engaged, fruitful member of a local, gospel-believing church. What does it mean to be deeply invested in your church? It means more than attendance, more than a decal on the back of your car, and more than a check in the offering plate.

In his letter to the church in Ephesus, the apostle Paul explains what it looks like when each member embraces God's call for them to minister within the church.

The Work of Ministry

> And he himself gave some to be apostles, some prophets, some evangelists, some pastors and teachers, to equip the saints for the work of ministry, to build up the body of Christ. (Eph. 4:11–12)

We most often hear the word *minister* to describe those who are paid by the church. When guests visit either of our churches, they sometimes ask who the minister of the church is. Though it's a common use of the term *minister*, it's not the most accurate. Those called to do the ministry are not just the vocational pastors, but the saints—that's all believers. All who have been saved by God's grace are called to the work of the ministry. As the apostle Paul argues in Ephesians 4, those who lead the church—the pastor/teachers—are not called to do all the ministry, but to equip the saints to do the ministry. For Paul, the primary function of pastors is to train the members to serve.

Churches have often looked at pastors as bus drivers when they should view them as driving instructors. For instance, when traveling to summer cap, a bus driver always drives the bus. He's not responsible for teaching children to drive. In fact, he'll lose his job if he lets a student get behind the wheel. His only responsibility is to get the students safely from point A to point B, from the stop to the camp. The kids aren't responsible for learning how to drive the bus. They don't do any work on the bus, but just sit there and go for a ride until it's time to get off.

Doesn't that sound like a lot of churches? Come, take a seat, let the professionals do the work, get up, and leave. Yet pastors aren't bus drivers, but driving instructors. The duty of a driving instructor isn't to taxi the students safely from one place to another. A driving instructor teaches his students to drive themselves. He trains them how to drive safely and skillfully. His job is to equip them to do the work of driving.

A healthy church doesn't view the pastors as bus drivers. Pastors are not called to their office to do ministry. They do ministry because they are Christians. They are called to the pastoral role to teach and train. To put it another way, the pastor's primary ministry is to equip the members to do the work of the ministry.

One reason many churches have ignored this pattern and handed over the work of ministry to the paid staff is because the biblical pattern demands more time, effort, and commitment from the members. The members would rather sit comfortably and watch the pastors than get involved themselves.

In a healthy church, the pastors are like personal trainers, teaching the members how to exercise, showing them the correct methods, and challenging them to greater commitment. But the members are the ones responsible to get out of bed early, drive to the gym, lift the weights, and push themselves to grow stronger.

Ministry requires strength and commitment because it's hard work. The word for *ministry* is preceded by the description *work* and reveals the nature of what Jesus wants us to do as part of His church. He wants His people to work hard—often behind the scenes, without recognition or reward. In a different letter, the apostle Paul encourages church members to abound in the Lord's work, because their labor will not be in vain.[2] Apart from Labor Day, we don't use that word to describe something fun or pleasant. *Labor* gives the impression of something that will exhaust us and leave us weary.

What God is calling each church member to do is to put on their hard hat, pick up their lunch pail, and get busy. Each member is called to wake up and see the needs before them, clock in, and use their energy to work toward the advancement of God's kingdom. When you think of your role in your church, you should think about the different ways God wants you to work hard.

In case we doubt the amount of effort required, we should remember the example of Jesus, who came not to be ministered to, but to minister to others.[3] We serve others like Jesus served us. Though this should encourage us to work hard in ministry, it can feel discouraging. Maybe you already hear the doubts and excuses: "I can't minister like Jesus. I can't give myself to others like He has given Himself for me. It's impossible." But we can minister like Jesus because He gives us the grace necessary to serve others.[4] We embrace the position of servant because of the grace we've received. Our ministry is empowered by Jesus Himself. His Spirit is at work in us to produce effective ministry through us.

It doesn't matter how gifted your pastors are; no one member of the church has all the spiritual gifts necessary to singlehandedly do the ministry of the church. This is why the Spirit gifts each member of the church for ministry in order to build up the body of Christ.

When you think about your role in the church, are you a minister or a consumer? Companies view us as consumers and spend millions influencing us to consume more and more of their product. We often bring the same mindset into the church, looking for what we like, what we want, what we think we need. But Jesus calls us to see our role in the church as a minister, not a consumer. We don't attend just to get more of something, but to give of ourselves for the good of others and the glory of our Lord.

Viewing yourself as a minister changes how you engage in the ministries of the church. There will be nights when you don't feel like attending your small group, just as there are days you don't feel like going to work. But the knowledge that God has called you to the hard work of ministry can help you go, with a mind to minister to others, even on those nights when it's tough.

The Method of Ministry

> But speaking the truth in love, let us grow in every way into him who is the head—Christ. From him the whole body, fitted and knit together by every supporting ligament, promotes the growth of the body for building itself up in love by the proper working of each individual part. (Eph. 4:15–16)

When we think about the work of ministry, our minds might drift to cleaning a church bathroom, changing a dirty diaper, carrying furniture from the U-Haul into the house, or making a meal. But there's a more difficult and challenging way for us to do the work of ministry. Our method for ministry is to speak truth to other members in love. For some of us (maybe most of us), that's a lot more difficult and taxing than crawling around on the floor with a toddler. Speaking the truth in love takes more effort, sacrifice, and discipline than setting up a table in the lobby. Speaking the truth in love is often hard, messy, dirty work.

The phrase "speaking the truth" in verse 15 is one word in the original language. It's the word *truth* turned into a verb. Members are to be *truthing* each other in love. Your relationship with those in the body should be characterized by truthing one another. In 1978, Billy Joel released a song called "Honesty" lamenting the difficulty of finding anyone who tells the truth. Truth is a precious commodity in our world because it's so rare. If Christians won't share the truth with one another, who will? The number one way you can minister to your brothers and sisters is by truthing them—by speaking the truth into their lives.

But notice the way we speak the truth to others is qualified. Our attitude in speaking the truth is one of love. Sometimes we think of love and truth as enemies. We think it's unloving to share the truth, or we think it's loving to avoid a certain topic. Though they're hard to balance, truth and love go hand in hand. Love is no enemy of the truth. We're reminded of this in Proverbs 27:5: "Better an open reprimand than concealed love." It's unloving to remain silent when something needs to be said. Though the truth may sting, it's loving to share it if it serves someone's greater good. It's not unlike the work of a good surgeon. A good surgeon cuts, but cuts to heal. Both the action and the intent are important. As Tim Chester says, "Love without truth is like doing heart surgery with a wet fish. But truth without love is like doing heart surgery with a hammer."[5] Or, as the old saying goes, "Truth without love is brutality, but love without truth is hypocrisy."

Life in this world is hard. We're constantly bombarded by lies. Television, movies, and magazines present an illusion of reality. But it's an airbrushed, photoshopped, edited, computer-generated version. We each need a place where we can hear the truth spoken into our lives. That place is the community of faith—the church. But we need to hear it more than just on Sundays. We hear lies all week long, so we need to hear the truth more often. We need others truthing us throughout the week.

This is how church members minister to one another. We meet together as part of our lives to hear the truth. We need a refuge from the bombardment of worldly deception, and we find it in relationships with brothers and sisters in the church. All of us need this—none of us are exempt. We need others to look out for us and to protect us by truthing us. The writer to the Hebrews warns us:

> Watch out, brothers and sisters, so that there won't be in any of you an evil, unbelieving heart that turns away from the living God. But encourage each other daily, while it is still called today, so that none of you is hardened by sin's deception. (Heb. 3:12–13)

Every single one of us is in danger of falling away from the living God. Our hearts can grow hard, and hardness is the result of the deceitfulness of sin. Sin doesn't announce its presence. It doesn't come with a marching band. Sin is a ninja, a commando, an assault team lying in ambush. We don't see sin until it's too late. That's why we need others speaking the truth into our lives.

Do you see how we all need to hear the truth and be speaking the truth? That's why in our churches the members make this promise to each other in the church covenant: We will walk with our brothers and sisters in love, exercising an affectionate care and watchfulness over our fellow believers. We minister to each other by watching over each other's souls, and we do that by regularly and consistently speaking the truth into each other's lives.

There are many ways to accomplish this as a church. Not only small groups, but also Bible studies, prayer times, and fellowships. You will get out of them only what you put into them. If you attend infrequently or sit in the corner with your arms folded and your mouth closed, they won't be that helpful to you. Even more, you won't be helpful to others. But if you engage, if you share your struggles and invite others to speak into your life, and if you do the same for them in return, you will see God work.

The Goal of Ministry

> To equip the saints for the work of ministry, to build up the body of Christ, until we all reach unity in the faith and in the knowledge of God's Son, growing into maturity with a stature measured by Christ's fullness. Then we will no longer be little children, tossed by the waves and blown around by every wind

> of teaching, by human cunning with cleverness in the techniques of deceit. But speaking the truth in love, let us grow in every way into him who is the head—Christ. From him the whole body, fitted and knit together by every supporting ligament, promotes the growth of the body for building itself up in love by the proper working of each individual part. (Eph. 4:12–16)

The goal of member-to-member ministry is a church that is growing in maturity. This happens as members serve one another by speaking the truth of Jesus Christ into each other's lives. As we faithfully serve each other this way, we begin to think the same true things about the Faith, and we grow in our understanding of Jesus Christ and in our relationship to Him.

God's goal for each one of His children is conformity to the image of Jesus Christ. Romans 8 says He foreknew, predestined, called, and justified us so that one day we would fully be conformed to the image of His Son.[6] The way He's accomplishing this is through the church—through the ministry of other Christians. Individually and corporately, we are being changed into the likeness of Jesus Christ. We are thinking more like Him, acting more like Him, loving more like Him, and becoming more like Him.

As this happens, we stop acting like spiritual children, but grow up into mature manhood.[7] It's hard to define *manhood*, but you know it when you see it. We've all seen two guys the same age, and one strikes us as a man and the other as a boy. The way they act, talk, and view life—one has started to get it and the other still doesn't.

Church members need to help each other get it. We need to help each other handle the ups and downs of life with maturity instead of throwing a temper tantrum. We need to protect each other from those who would take advantage of the weak and immature in our midst. We need to care deeply for the spiritual growth and maturity of those around us.

If you identify areas of immaturity in another member—whether theological, spiritual, social, or ethical—you have a responsibility to engage them with the goal of helping them mature. It's important for you to keep the goal in mind—you're trying to help grow into greater maturity. Beating someone over the head with a Bible rarely helps them mature. Loving and patiently walking with them and helping them understand the truth and pushing them to greater love for Christ will help them grow up into Him.

There's always room for a church to grow in maturity because our goal is to reach the measure of the height of the fullness of Christ.[8] No church should ever be content with their current level of maturity, but should always be pushing, always growing, always progressing. Ultimately, spiritual maturity is a group project. It happens within the church as each member engages in the lives of their fellow members. This is why we see so many "one another commands" throughout the New Testament.

- Love one another
- Honor one another
- Be devoted to one another

- Live in harmony with one another
- Accept one another
- Instruct one another
- Agree with one another
- Serve one another
- Be patient with one another
- Forgive one another
- Admonish one another
- Encourage one another
- Be hospitable to one another
- Show kindness to one another

We don't care how mature you think you are, how many Bible verses you can recite—show us your maturity by how you care for others in the church. Jesus said that people would know His disciples by their love for each other.[9] What does your love for others in your church reveal about your spiritual maturity? We're not asking about your Bible knowledge; we're asking about your care for others. Are you helping your church body grow to be more like Christ by investing in the lives of the other members? You cannot keep the "one anothers" of the New Testament apart from commitment to a local church family.

The Investment of Ministry

You need unhurried opportunities to engage in ministering to others in your church. Many churches have small groups or Sunday school classes to provide an opportunity for member-to-member ministry. These groups are not the only way, but they are an important way. But let us give you a warning: Signing up for a small group guarantees nothing. Neither does showing up at that small group. Small groups are merely a context to engage in your responsibility to care for others in the body. You have to take the initiative. You have to do the work. If you've never attempted to minister to other members, it can seem difficult and intimidating. You may not know how to get started.

You start by investing time and effort into building relationships. Why is our default thinking that relationships are easy and don't take any work? Building quality relationships takes planning and effort. When a young man is interested in dating a young lady, it rarely just happens, no matter what the latest rom-com claims. First, he thinks about it, then strategizes, before finally putting a plan into action. Relationships take effort and intention. Don't assume they will just happen. Figure out how to spend time with other people and think ahead of time about questions you might ask. Take responsibility to get to know another person.

You might be thinking. *I'm too shy. I'm socially awkward. I don't know where to begin.* Here's some advice: Ask them questions about their life. Most people like to talk about themselves. If you'll ask them and then listen, most people will share. Some won't, initially. All that means is you'll need to roll up your sleeves and work harder. In time, the more you learn about someone the better prompting questions you can ask, and in turn, get to know them better. In order to build relationships, you have to invest time and effort in conversations.

Within that relationship, you need to talk about what really matters. Honest and open conversation can be awkward, especially at first. But like anything, it gets easier the more you do it. Bring up spiritual matters in your conversations. After the church service on Sunday, ask someone else what they learned from the sermon. Have them elaborate. Dig a little deeper. Be willing to share how God challenged you through the songs, Scripture readings, and preaching. Ask probing questions. Don't settle for bland, surface answers. Assure them that when you ask, "How are you doing?" you really want to know.

Invite them over for dinner and tell them beforehand that you want to hear what God is doing in their life. Tell them about something you've read and the impact it's made on you. Ask for their input into your sins and struggles. Don't avoid meaningful conversations—seek them out! Investing time and effort in your conversations will produce tremendous fruit in your relationships.

The type of "one another" care seen in the New Testament demands deep relationships. It will not come if you only swim in the shallow end of relationships. The hard work of building relationships stands behind the command to Christians in 1 Thessalonians 5:14: "And we exhort you, brothers and sisters: warn those who are idle, comfort the discouraged, help the weak, be patient with everyone." You won't know who's idle, who's fainthearted, and who's weak until you've invested time and effort building deep relationships.

Conclusion

For you to build deep relationships, you need to be willing to open up your own life. That's scary. For many of us that's the real reason we don't invest time and effort in relationships. We're scared of people knowing us. If that's your fear, then you need—we want to stress this—you need to invite people in. You're in a dangerous place. Your sin is telling you to keep people away. Your sin is telling you to keep the walls up. Your sin is telling you that God's wrong, and you really don't need others. We all need other believers. We need to know and be known. So, invest time and effort in conversations that build deeper relationships.

If you're not a church member, then your first step is to find a church that preaches the gospel and join it. Commit yourself to other Christians. Member-to-member ministry can only be carried out in the context of a local church. If you are a church member, Jesus has called you to minister to the other members of your church by speaking the truth in love so that together you grow up to be more like Jesus. Do it. Be active. Be faithful. Be engaged. Get to work for the glory of Christ and the health of His body.

Chapter Four

Every Member a Servant

Now concerning spiritual gifts: brothers and sisters, I do not want you to be unaware. You know that when you were pagans, you used to be enticed and led astray by mute idols. Therefore I want you to know that no one speaking by the Spirit of God says, "Jesus is cursed," and no one can say, "Jesus is Lord," except by the Holy Spirit. Now there are different gifts, but the same Spirit. There are different ministries, but the same Lord. And there are different activities, but the same God works all of them in each person. A manifestation of the Spirit is given to each person for the common good: to one is given a message of wisdom through the Spirit, to another, a message of knowledge by the same Spirit, to another, faith by the same Spirit, to another, gifts of healing by the one Spirit, to another, the performing of miracles, to another, prophecy, to another, distinguishing between spirits, to another, different kinds of tongues, to another, interpretation of tongues. One and the same Spirit is active in all these, distributing to each person as he wills.

1 Corinthians 12:1–11

Many colleges and universities have two types of sports: intercollegiate and intramural. The intercollegiate teams officially represent the school when playing against other universities. Intramural sports are all "in-house." They're like a rec league for young adults.

Every year, students try out for the intercollegiate team, but only a few of the top athletes make it. After all, most of the slots on these teams are already filled by athletes on scholarship. There are always those former high school standouts who try out for the intercollegiate team with the hope of earning a spot on the roster. When they are cut, it's not easy. It's challenging to go from being the go-to star on your high school team one year to being a spectator the next.

For this reason, intramural teams are a great outlet for those with failed sports dreams. After all, no one gets cut from an intramural team. The more people who sign up, the more teams you have. But intramural sports are a lot different than intercollegiate sports. A number of things are optional, like experience, skill, and being in shape. For this reason, intramural sports allow those high school stars to become stars once again.

Imagine a former high school star—now an intramural basketball player—who plays weekly against other players with little ability. Most likely, his star regains some luster, and he begins to shine. As the intramural season progresses, he becomes the go-to scorer again, averaging 30 or 40 points in a game. He rarely pass the ball. But no one minds. When he carries the team, it usually leads to a win.

You can imagine what might happen when students start to compare the intramural player to those on the intercollegiate team. "He's better than half of the guys on the team." "If he was on the team, they would have won that last game." "I don't understand why he didn't make the team." "With the way our intercollegiate team is playing, I think he could start right now!"

But the grumbling intramural experts don't understand that this star stood out during intercollegiate tryouts for all the wrong reasons. If they were to talk to the coaches, they'd find out that he's not on the team because his abilities don't help the team. He might be talented, but he's selfish and lazy. In intercollegiate sports, a player's ability is measured by how it helps a team, not by how it looks in highlights. Your abilities are only as good as their impact on the team.

It's not much different in the church. You see, God, through His Spirit, gives each church member a gift, but these gifts are only valuable as they serve the church's good. The Spirit empowers each member to serve other members. The effectiveness of a member's gift is measured by its impact on others, not the attention it draws to them.

If the church is going to fulfill its mission, every member matters. That's why every member needs to understand their role as a servant. Members using their gifts to serve the body allow the entire body to grow healthy and strong.

The Spirit's Presence

> Now concerning spiritual gifts: brothers and sisters, I do not want you to be unaware. You know that when you were pagans, you used to be enticed and led astray by mute idols. Therefore I want you to know that no one speaking by the Spirit of God says, "Jesus is

> cursed," and no one can say, "Jesus is Lord,"
> except by the Holy Spirit. (1 Cor. 12:1–3)

Chapter 12 is the first of three chapters in 1 Corinthians that focus on spiritual gifts. There are many views on spiritual gifts, but the primary point of these chapters is not to argue for or against the presence of certain spiritual gifts in the modern church. Instead, the intention is to demonstrate the purpose of spiritual gifts as a whole.

The apostle Paul begins his lengthy discussion of spiritual gifts by reminding the church that all true believers are indwelt by the Holy Spirit. Understanding the gifts starts with clearly articulating the Spirit's active role in each believer's life.

Paul contrasts the believer's life before salvation and his life after salvation. Before salvation, each one of us was being led by mute idols. Whether it was a literal idol on a shelf or an invisible idol of the heart, all of us were taking orders from gods that lack the ability to speak. Paul is employing sarcasm to expose the insanity of basing your decisions on the whims of lifeless gods who have no power to communicate. How can a piece of wood lead a person? How can carved stone give commands or offer comfort? No wonder life without Jesus Christ is doomed. No wonder there is no hope in idolatry. In idolatry, a person takes orders from a god who cannot talk. In contrast, a believer is led by the Holy Spirit, who leads us away from mute idols to the living Christ. The Holy Spirit speaks through us to say, "Jesus is Lord."

The fundamental distinction between Christians and non-Christians is their view of Jesus Christ. A Christian submits to the lordship of Jesus Christ, and an unbeliever doesn't. In the book of Romans, Paul talks about how a person becomes a Christian. He writes, "If you confess with your mouth, 'Jesus is Lord,' and believe in your heart that God raised him from the dead, you will be saved. One believes with the heart, resulting in righteousness, and one confesses with the mouth, resulting in salvation" (10:9–10). A Christian confesses that Jesus is Lord.

These are not magical words but the cry of a heart ready and willing to gladly submit everything to Jesus. "Jesus is Lord" means He is the master and commander of your destiny. "Jesus is Lord" means He has been given the throne of your heart. "Jesus is Lord" means you have sworn allegiance to Him as your King. "Jesus is Lord" means you have given up the right to live for yourself. "Jesus is Lord" is the desperate plea of the one who has reached the end of themselves. "Jesus is Lord" is a cry for help, for Jesus to guide and govern you for the rest of your life and the life beyond. "Jesus is Lord" is what it means to be a Christian.

Have you ever confessed that Jesus is Lord? You submit to someone as lord of your life—everyone does. Who is it? You can attempt to be the lord of your own life, but that will fail miserably and end in destruction. If you are the lord of your life, you have assumed control. But you're not in control. You have no control over your health or the length of your life. You have no control over disaster or drought. You make a miserable lord over your life.

Submit to Jesus as Lord. Jesus Christ, the Son of God, became a man and died in the place of sinful mankind. Our rebellion from God, our desire for lordship, is punishable by death. But Jesus died in our place. He took our punishment, and then He rose from the dead. He is now reigning from the throne room of heaven. At some point in the future, He will return, and everyone will confess that He is Lord. Those who gladly confess it will join Him in eternal joy. Those who obstinately refused to confess Him as Lord will suffer His just and holy wrath. In the end, everyone will bow their knees to Jesus, some in worshipful gratitude and others in absolute terror. If you are not a Christian, we urge you to put down this book, repent of your rebellion, and then confess Him as Lord. Yield your allegiance to Him. Pledge your life to Him.

Confessing Jesus as Lord happens when the Holy Spirit leads a person from rebellion to submission. Everyone who confesses Jesus as Lord does so because of the Spirit of God at work in them. Throughout this letter, Paul reminds the church that the Holy Spirit lives inside each Christian.[1] Every genuine believer has the Spirit of God dwelling within. The Spirit is the One who led them from idolatry to worship Jesus Christ, so no true believer is without the Spirit.

A Variety of Gifts

> Now there are different gifts, but the same Spirit. There are different ministries, but the same Lord. And there are different activities, but the same God works all of them in each person. (1 Cor. 12:4–6)

Having established that all believers are indwelt by the Spirit, the apostle Paul now turns to spiritual gifts. This one Spirit, who indwells all believers, gives various gifts. Again, he stresses that all believers share in the same Spirit. To further drive that point home, he brings in all three members of the Godhead—the Father, Son, and Holy Spirit. We share the same Spirit (v. 4), the same Lord (v. 5), and the same God (v. 6).

Unity of belief, but diversity of function. We all follow the same Lord through the ministry of the same Spirit to fulfill the will of the same God, but we do so in different ways as the Spirit gifts each of us. The word *gift* is the Greek word *charisma*. The root of which is *charis*, meaning "grace." These are gifts of grace given by the Holy Spirit so that we can serve each other. Notice how the text goes back and forth from diversity to unity.

- Verse 4—A variety of gifts, but the same Spirit.
- Verse 5—A variety of services, but the same Lord.
- Verse 6—A variety of activities, but the same God.

One God gives a variety of gifts to His people. God's definition of unity always includes diversity. God's unity is not uniformity—where all distinction is denied. One author suggests the unity God desires for a church is like the unity of a blizzard.[2] When you look at the snow falling, it's a picture of unity. Snowflake after snowflake falls to the ground, making a blanket of pure white. If you go out into the snow and grab a handful, it compresses together to create a single snowball. The pristine covering of white snow is a beautiful picture of unity. Yet, each snowflake is different. No two snowflakes are the same—each uniquely designed by God. Unity in diversity.

Most of the time, our feeble attempts at unity are less like snowflakes and more like ice cubes—each one exactly the same, with as little difference as possible. Biblical unity is not uniformity. It's not a legion of faceless, nameless storm troopers or a swarm of mindless drones. Unity exists most beautifully in diversity.

There can be a tendency in churches to think that unity will best be achieved by flattening out all gifts and abilities. If we make every member do exactly the same thing at exactly the same time in exactly the same way, then we will achieve unity. Unity is not the result of equal gifting. It's the result of every single member receiving their gifts from the same God.

The Same Purpose

> A manifestation of the Spirit is given to each person for the common good. (1 Cor. 12:7)

Unity is not only the result of receiving our gifts from the same God but also of using our gifts for the same purpose. The Spirit demonstrates His power through you for the benefit of the entire church. He empowers you to serve the common good. Real unity in the church comes as each member submits themselves to the same Lord and commits themselves to serving each other.

The main difference between the intramural star and those who play on the college basketball team is more profound than the uniform they wear to their games. Those intramural stars play in such a way to draw attention to themselves—for their own good. However, players on a college team often sacrifice personal statistics and achievements to achieve a common goal. They work to make the team successful. Each person is willing to play the role that best serves the team. They are united in a common purpose.

Throughout his first letter, the apostle Paul constantly pushes the Corinthian church away from self-centeredness. If this letter were a song, the chorus would be about selfless sacrifice. We hear the same notes over and over throughout 1 Corinthians. Here are just a few examples:

> Now I urge you, brothers and sisters, in the name of our Lord Jesus Christ, that all of you agree in what you say, that there be no divisions among you, and that you be united with the same understanding and the same conviction. (1 Cor. 1:10)

> As it is, to have legal disputes against one another is already a defeat for you. Why not rather be wronged? Why not rather be cheated? Instead, you yourselves do wrong and cheat—and you do this to brothers and sisters! (1 Cor. 6:7–8)

> But be careful that this right of yours in no way becomes a stumbling block to the weak. . . . Therefore, if food causes my brother or sister to fall, I will never again eat meat, so that I won't cause my brother or sister to fall. (1 Cor. 8:9, 13)

> Although I am free from all and not anyone's slave, I have made myself a slave to everyone, in order to win more people. . . . Now I do all this because of the gospel, so that I may share in the blessings. (1 Cor. 9:19, 23)

> No one is to seek his own good, but the good of the other person. (1 Cor. 10:24)

God is commanding His people to engage outside of their bubble. Many people live each day as if a bubble surrounds them, and the only thing that has meaning is what penetrates the bubble. Their bubble is a mini planet around which others revolve, a way of looking at every situation and the first question is, "How does this affect me?" Life in the bubble becomes a way of protecting yourself from anything that would hamper your own plans. Life in the bubble allows you to focus, if not exclusively, primarily on what you want to accomplish.

God did not create you to live in a protective bubble. God created you, and if you're a Christian, He saved you and equipped you to live a life of service to others. You need to regularly ask yourself, "Am I living in a bubble right now? Am I only concerned with what impacts me? Am I stepping out from my bubble to engage in the lives of my fellow members?" If you discover that you're in the bubble, step out of the bubble and get busy serving someone else. Put aside your agenda and focus on the common good. Every believer is gifted to serve the body in some way, and that includes you. God has given you a gift in order to serve others. It's a gift of grace, and it should be used as a funnel of grace. His grace should flow through you in service to someone else.

Evangelical Christianity is plagued by an epidemic of selfishness. Too often, Christians are devoted to their own plans and committed to accomplishing their own goals. We have become consumers, evaluating the church based on what it can do for us. The same consumer mindset can even influence how we think about using the gifts and abilities God has given us. We can view church as a means to self-fulfillment. "What church will allow me to use my gifts in the way I want to?" Can you hear the apostle Paul sigh in frustration and then say to us, "Get over yourself. It's not about you. God didn't equip you to make a name for yourself. He didn't give you gifts to make you feel better. God equips people to serve others. It's not about you!" Why do you serve? If you help in the nursery or hand out bulletins or serve as a deacon or teach a class, why do you do it? Are you motivated by the needs of others or are you hoping to find self-fulfillment in a ministry position?

In this passage, we could broadly define a spiritual gift as a "divinely empowered ability to meet the need of another with grace." How can anything that revolves around grace be self-centered? No word pictures "selflessness" like the word *grace*. Grace is receiving something we don't deserve. How could we selfishly turn around and use a gift of grace to accomplish our own plans? The Spirit of God equips us to serve others, not our own agendas.

A List of Gifts

> To one is given a message of wisdom through the Spirit, to another, a message of knowledge by the same Spirit, to another, faith by the same Spirit, to another, gifts of healing by the one Spirit, to another, the performing of miracles, to another, prophecy, to another, distinguishing between spirits, to another, different kinds of tongues, to another, interpretation of tongues. One and the same Spirit is active in all these, distributing to each person as he wills. (1 Cor. 12:8–11)

The Spirit indwells all believers and gives each believer a gift or multiple gifts to minister grace to others. The apostle Paul lists a number of spiritual gifts, but his purpose is not to make a definitive catalog. Later in this chapter, Paul mentions other gifts not mentioned here.[3] The main point of this list is to illustrate the diversity of God's gifts of grace. Look at that list again. It's quite a list. From healing to tongues, prophecy to miracles, it's one diverse list. Which is precisely Paul's point. The Spirit empowers believers to serve others, and He does so in whatever way at whatever moment best suits His purpose.

We should ask why he selects these gifts in this section. What do these particular gifts have in common? Is there something significant about this selection of gifts? He chooses what we would consider the most miraculous of the gifts, the most astounding and extraordinary. Why highlight the most noticeable? Because all gifts are given to serve others, even the ones that draw attention. He highlights the gifts most likely to draw attention and says, "Even these, especially these, are given by the Spirit to serve others."

How easy it would be to make miracle-working about us. If you could work miracles, you might be tempted to hold rallies and sell tickets, to see your name in lights, and to play in sold-out arenas. This list is a reminder that no gifts are given to glorify the one who receives the gift. They are gifts of grace. They are divinely empowered abilities to meet the needs of another with grace.

This instruction section ends with a simple, powerful summary of how spiritual gifts are intended to help members serve one another within the church. In verse 11, we see the variety of gifts in the words "all these." We see the unity of identity and purpose in the words "empowered by one and the same Spirit." Then we see a final important reminder—"as He wills." God is sovereign. He knows what's best, and He decides who receives what gifts. Everyone is gifted by God to serve, but not everyone will serve in the same way.

Serving with Spiritual Gifts

Remember, God has called all Christians to serve others with the spiritual gifts he has given us. On every successful basketball team, the players figure out each other's roles and abilities. They don't figure this out by standing on the sidelines taking a quiz but by playing together on the court. As the players run up and down, they realize who can dribble and who can't. Who can shoot, and who should pass instead. Who can rebound and set picks. You're not going to discover how God has gifted you to serve in your church until you get in the game.

You are probably familiar with the "spiritual gifts" tests found online. If you answer the questions right, you can receive affirmation for whatever spiritual gifts you want. You can fill out page after page of spiritual gift inventories, but those usually only tell you what you like to do in theory. They don't tell you how God might plan to use you in the real world. But God has given us a better way! The best way to figure out what your gifts are is to start serving other members. Spend time with other members in the church, figure out what their needs are, and start trying to meet them. Even more, other members will begin to affirm the gifts that God has actually given you!

A healthy church doesn't select its leaders hoping they'll start leading. Instead, they recognize deacons who already care for the widows and orphans. They appoint elders who already shepherd the flock of God. They don't see a person's natural abilities and appoint them to a role hoping they'll fulfill it, but instead, recognize a person's gifts as they serve others.

Your gifts become obvious as you serve others. One author wrote that your gifts "are not for individual enjoyment, but for corporate employment."[4] The word *employment* brings to mind a soldier who uses his talent and training to serve his country. He sacrifices his own needs for the benefit of others. He does whatever is necessary for his squad to return safely. Are you employed in serving others? Are you working for the common good of the church? Do you look for opportunities to engage in ministering to the needs of the other members? When was the last time you were aware of another member's need? How did you take steps to meet it?

Aren't you thankful for how God designed the church? Like snowflakes, we are all unique. God designed each one of us to be distinct. That means others will be gifted differently than you. That's okay. In fact, that's better than okay. That's great! What would your church be like if every member shared the same set of skills? It would be a church with serious problems. Thank God for the different gifts and abilities He has given your church. Don't be envious of others' gifts. Be grateful. The best basketball teams have people with wildly different skill sets working in harmony. A church is most effective in its mission when each member uses the diverse gifts God has given them in harmony.

Conclusion

Everyone in the church loved Dewey, so the room was full when he started a new class at the church. But over time, the attendance dwindled. In class, people often asked for clarification or more explanation as he taught. He initially assumed it was a deficiency in their understanding. But, over time, he saw that he didn't have the gifts to be a teacher. However, the pastors knew the church family's affection for Dewey. So, they encouraged him to hand the class off to someone else and reassigned him to lead visitation teams. Both Dewey and the visitation ministry flourished because Dewey humbly used his gifts for the common good.

Pastor Justin returned from his two-month leave with some trepidation. After four long years of church planting, he was thankful the church was established and doing well. He was also thankful that the church leadership had recognized his need for time away to rest and to care for his aging parents. He was excited to be back preaching, but he was worried about how the church would look. When he left, he was involved in every aspect of church life, from selecting curriculum in the children's classes to organizing the trailers that held all their equipment. Whenever there was a question about anything, people looked to Pastor Justin for the answer.

Walking back in the doors of the rented school, Justin was pleasantly surprised by how organized everything appeared. The chaos he had envisioned was absent. The closer he looked, the more he realized everything was more organized than when he left. Instead of asking how things were going, he stepped quietly into the shadows and watched. Before long, he realized that the set-up crew looked to Ryan, a fairly new member of the church, for instruction. Ryan had come to the church after retiring from the Army, where he had spent his career in logistics. Apparently if Ryan could handle supplying an army in combat, he could also handle leading a team to set up and store equipment. In that moment, Justin realized that his time away not only blessed him with rest and refreshment, but it also opened up space for others to use their gifts to serve the church.

God assigns spiritual gifts as He wills to whom He wills. And while all gifts are not equally visible, they are equally important. No one member of the church has all the spiritual gifts. We need each other. There is no gift your church needs that God has not given to one of the members, so get busy using your gifts to serve other members, thanking God for His wisdom in uniquely preparing and empowering each member in your church for His glory and the good of the church.

Chapter Five

Every Member a Disciple-Maker

You, therefore, my son, be strong in the grace that is in Christ Jesus. What you have heard from me in the presence of many witnesses, commit to faithful men who will be able to teach others also.
2 Timothy 2:1–2

Language differences make for some good laughs. Two local men were serving as cooks for a visiting American youth group on their mission trip to Africa. When they heard the students talk about eating "chicken fingers," they started laughing uncontrollably. They couldn't understand why chicken strips were called "chicken fingers." After all, chickens don't have fingers.

Sometimes, the difference in language can be instructive. Pastors in Moldova refer to the men they're training in their church as "their disciples." We have never heard an American pastor use that phrase. Imagine if you saw one of your Christian friends at a local restaurant with a table of people you had never met before. Your friend introduced the group by saying, "These are my disciples." You might wonder if your friend had fallen off the deep end and started a cult. "My disciples?" We don't typically think or talk like this, do we? But maybe we should. After all, that's the term Jesus used for His followers.

Jesus's disciples were His students of life, His apprentices in day-to-day living. You might be thinking, *Well, that was Jesus.* Remember that Jesus instructed His disciples to "go and make disciples." His command reminds us of the importance of discipleship. Maybe changing our terminology would remind us that part of the job of every disciple is to make new disciples. Church membership is about more than committing to attend the same church each Sunday. If you're simply a spectator each week, we want to see you get off the sidelines, join the team, and enter the game.

In the previous chapters, we've seen every member's role in the church's mission. How every member is a worshipper, a minister, and a servant. Hopefully, you've considered each of these areas. Let's assume you have. You're a member fully committed to God's work through His church. You worship, minister, and serve with a sweet spirit. There's more. It's time to think about discipleship.

Committed disciples train new disciples. Every disciple is called to be a disciple-maker. You've seen how this works if you've ever been on a team or part of a band. The upperclassmen help the underclassmen. The veterans coach the rookies. The seasoned employee trains the newbies. You're not done when you're a fully committed disciple of Jesus Christ yourself. You're just getting started. Now, you're in a perfect position to help disciple someone else.

If you've learned how to worship, teach someone else. If you've learned how to minister, show someone else. If you've learned how to serve, find someone who hasn't, come alongside them, and disciple them. The apostle Paul's second letter to Timothy emphasizes the importance of disciples training disciples.

Discipleship as Example

> You, therefore, my son, be strong in the grace that is in Christ Jesus. What you have heard from me in the presence of many witnesses, commit to faithful men who will be able to teach others also. (2 Tim. 2:1–2)

For the second time in this letter, the apostle Paul refers to Timothy as "his child" (2 Tim. 1:2 ESV). He begins his first letter to Timothy similarly: "To Timothy, my true son in the faith" (1 Tim. 1:2). Timothy is not Paul's physical descendant. Paul is not his birth father or even adopted father. Paul is his father in the faith. He considers Timothy his spiritual son. Because of this, Paul takes responsibility for Timothy's spiritual growth.

But it's not just Timothy! Paul has other spiritual children as well. He calls Titus his "true child in a common faith" (1:4 ESV), and he says the church in the ancient city of Corinth is made up of his "beloved children" (1 Cor. 4:14 ESV). Listen to what he says:

> I'm not writing this to shame you, but to warn you as my dear children. For you may have countless instructors in Christ, but you don't have many fathers. For I became your father in Christ Jesus through the gospel. Therefore I urge you to imitate me. This is why I have sent

> Timothy to you. He is my dearly loved and faithful child in the Lord. He will remind you about my ways in Christ Jesus, just as I teach everywhere in every church. (1 Cor. 4:14–17)

They are Paul's "children" because he is responsible for their growth and development. They heard the gospel from him, responded to it, watched his life, and began to grow and mature. Like a father, he watched over them and discipled them from the very moment they were born spiritually.

To a different church, he likened his relationship to them to that between a mother and her nursing child. He loved them, cared for them, watched over them, and gave up his comforts to see them grow, just like a mother does with her children.[1] So when he calls Timothy "his son," he means that he has invested his life in Timothy's spiritual growth and development. How did he do this? How did he invest in Timothy and these other Christians? How did he disciple them?

Listen to what he says in his letter to the Philippians: "Do what you have learned and received and heard from me, and seen in me, and the God of peace will be with you" (Phil. 4:9). He not only taught them about following Jesus but he also modeled for them what it means to follow Jesus. In other words, he's been a parent to them. Isn't this what parents do? We not only teach our kids, but we show them.

Many fathers with sons remember reaching a milestone in their family life—the last day they will have to mow their lawn. They have passed the mowing responsibilities on to their offspring, and once the sons are grown, they'll hire a neighborhood boy to take over. What does it look like for a father to train his son to mow the lawn? They can't just push him out into the yard, command him to mow the lawn, and close the garage door. No, they have to show him how to mow the lawn. The father has to demonstrate how to start the mower, where to mow, and how close the mower should get to trees and bushes. He watches his son closely the first couple of times he mows the lawn. He has to periodically stop him to show him something, like the one row with the tall grass he keeps missing. Eventually, after months of his son mowing, the father only has to tell him when to mow. Over time, he has learned what to do.

The apostle Paul not only tells Timothy and Titus how to follow Jesus but also shows them how to follow Jesus. That's what it means to disciple someone. As you read through the letters of the apostle Paul, you see him doing this all the time. He repeatedly tells Christians to remember what he has said and how he has lived. At least four different times, he says to imitate him.[2] He doesn't say it arrogantly—"Look how good I am." He says it like a father to his son—"Do it like I showed you. Imitate me." For someone to imitate you, they have to be close enough to see you. They have to be around you enough to know what you're like.

Imagine if students in a local high school made a video performing impressions of their teachers. A brand-new student comes to the school late in the year and walks into this viewing party on his first day. In the gathering, he finds hundreds of students howling in laughter. Each imitation causes them to laugh louder and louder. But the new student looks up at the screen, sees the video, and doesn't laugh, not even once. The reason is simple. He doesn't know the teachers, so the imitations don't make sense.

We can only imitate those we know. We can only imitate those we've seen and heard. The apostle Paul couldn't have said, "Imitate me," unless he made himself available to the members of these different churches. Before he instructed these Christians to follow him, he welcomed them into his life. Who have you welcomed into your life? Is there anyone who imitates you?

Over time, people imitate what they see you do more than what you tell them to do. More is caught than taught. The old proverb is correct: "Your walk talks, and your talk talks, but your walk talks louder than your talk talks." People will learn more from you if you bring them close enough to witness your behavior. The apostle Paul invited young Timothy into his life and began to disciple him to follow Jesus.

Discipleship as Instruction

> What you have heard from me in the presence of many witnesses, commit to faithful men who will be able to teach others also. (2 Tim. 2:2)

As he pens this letter, Paul knows the end of his life is advancing quickly. Later, he'll tell Timothy that he has just about finished his race.[3] Paul can see the finish line coming closer. He wants Timothy to think about the discipleship he's received from Paul and begin to disciple others.

Look at the pattern he lays out. Paul discipled Timothy. Timothy is supposed to disciple other faithful men, who will disciple others. Think of it like a relay team. Paul ran the first leg and then passed the baton to Timothy. Timothy is supposed to pass the baton to others, who will run their leg before passing it off again. But the race is more than four legs long—it's a never-ending relay race. Every stage is important. From Paul to Timothy, Timothy to faithful men, faithful men to others. If even one leg is missed, the results would be disastrous.

If you've ever installed a new chandelier in your home, you know they come with a long chain connected to the top in case it needs to be hung from a tall ceiling. Most ceilings are only eight or nine feet tall, but for some reason the manufacturer includes a chain suitable for Saint Peter's Basilica. In order to adjust the size of the chain, you have to remove some of the links. Removing a long length of chain isn't that difficult because all you need to do is pry open one link. Just one link and the rest of the chain comes off.

All Satan wants is to get rid of one link in the chain. If he could've gotten rid of Timothy, he could've gotten to all those faithful men and their followers. You're a link in the chain—has Satan gotten to you? Are there people you could reach who are currently disconnected from Jesus and His church because you're unwilling to invest in their lives? The chain has extended for 2,000 years as Christians have discipled the next generation to know and follow Christ. Let's not be the generation that breaks the chain.

This type of discipleship doesn't happen by chance. It has to be intentional. That's why Paul instructs Timothy to do it. If we assume it will just happen, we're naïve. We must see it as our responsibility to disciple others to follow Jesus. What other members of your church are you discipling? Who has God put around you? Who can you encourage to greater commitment to Jesus Christ?

Paul tells Timothy to commit the truth to faithful men. The word translated "commit" can also be translated "deposit." It's used that way in chapter 1, where Paul tells Timothy to "guard the good deposit" given to him (2 Tim. 1:14). Have you ever made a deposit by accident? One day you're driving around town doing errands, and you find yourself standing at the bank counter. "What just happened? How'd I get here? What should I do? Maybe I'll make a deposit." That's not how deposits happen. You plan to go to the bank. You write "bank" on your to-do list. When you arrive, you walk up to the teller and pass her your endorsed check. Making a deposit happens because you intentionally choose to make a deposit. Making a deposit to another Christian will only happen if you intentionally do it.

Some savvy seminary students might look at these verses and say, "Matt and Josh, these commands are directed to pastors. Timothy was a pastor and was being instructed to train other pastors. This doesn't apply to us non-pastors." You're right and wrong. The command is primarily referring to pastors, but not exclusively. Here's why.

Discipleship Is Expected

In his first letter to Timothy, Paul told him to be an example to the believers.[4] By commanding Timothy to train new disciples, the apostle Paul knows the church members will follow his example. They'll see Timothy and imitate him. This passage teaches "trickle-down discipleship." If the people at the top start training new disciples, it will trickle down from top to bottom, and those below them will do the same. If pastors disciple their members, the members will disciple other members. Pastors are examples of discipleship, but the call to disciple others is not exclusive to pastors. Every disciple is a disciple-maker.

In Titus 2, Paul instructs the older women to train the younger women.[5] He charges the older women to disciple the younger women to be godly women. In the same passage, Paul commands older men to have self-control and urges the younger men to follow their example, so the command to make disciples extends beyond pastors. His instructions raise a couple of questions: Who is an older man? Who is an older woman? Most church members are older than someone else in the church, right? Most of us fall into both categories: older and younger. We're older than some and younger than others. That means we need to learn from some and lead others.

The command to disciple is also given to parents. After commanding children to obey their parents, Paul tells fathers to bring up their children "in the discipline and instruction of the Lord" (Eph. 6:4 ESV). The word *discipline* shares the same root as *disciple*. Parents must train their children to know what God wants and how to follow Him.

We could look at many other examples in Scripture, but the point is simple. Each disciple is responsible for training new disciples. That's how Christianity spread from a dozen disciples in one Middle Eastern city to where we are now—millions of groups of disciples meeting in buildings around the globe 2,000 years later.

A great picture of discipleship is a graduation ceremony at a college that trains teachers. Those teachers were taught by teachers who were taught by teachers who were taught by teachers who were . . . you get the point. Hopefully, the students of these newly graduated teachers will teach their students, who will in turn teach their own students. Imagine what would happen if one generation decided not to participate. What would happen to education? If just one generation said, "Nah, we don't need to do that," the whole structure would collapse.

You see, God has chosen to call disciples one at a time. It's impossible to mass-produce disciples. Disciples aren't built-in factories; they're individually handcrafted. One disciple patiently pouring his life into another disciple, training them to follow Jesus. There is someone at your church that you can pour your life into right now. There is another member you can disciple in the faith. If you stop and think about it, someone's face may pop into your head as you read this. If you rack your brain and come up with no one, ask God to show you someone. If you ask, He'll make it clear. If you're thinking of someone right now but aren't sure how to get started, here are a couple of suggestions.

Start by saving someone a seat at church, though that might require you to give up your sacred buffer zone. Perhaps invite them over for dinner or out for lunch. Try inviting them to your small group or Sunday school class. That's a great place to pour yourself into another person. It's a custom-made opportunity to disciple them in the faith. As you meet each week to discuss God's Word and pray together, you'll get plenty of chances to help them grow. It's not that complicated, is it? However you choose to get started, remember this: Your spiritual growth is not an end in itself. You grow to help others grow. Your commitment isn't complete until you begin helping others commit to Christ.

Discipleship as Calling

> You, therefore, my son, be strong in the grace that is in Christ Jesus. (2 Tim. 2:1)

Making disciples may seem difficult, overwhelming, even impossible. Where do we get the ability to accomplish this Herculean feat? The power to disciple others comes from Jesus Christ. Before Timothy could instruct faithful men and be an example to believers, he needed to find his strength in the grace that comes only through Jesus Christ. This reminds us that God equips us for what He calls us to do.

This is the heart of Christianity. We cannot do what God has called us to do on our own, so our only hope is trusting in the grace that comes from Jesus Christ. We cannot please God or come to Him. He has to come to us through His Son, extending completely undeserved favor. In the previous chapter, Paul describes the grace that is at work in the life of a Christian.

> He has saved us and called us with a holy calling, not according to our works, but according to his own purpose and grace, which was given to us in Christ Jesus before time began. This has now been made evident through the appearing of our Savior Christ Jesus, who has abolished death and has brought life and immortality to light through the gospel. (2 Tim. 1:9–10)

The grace we have comes not from our works but directly from Jesus Christ. It was seen most clearly when Jesus died in our place and rose victorious from the dead. That grace rescues

Christians from death and makes them alive with God. Now, Paul says, that same grace empowers you to go to a fellow church member and invest your life in them. Just as Jesus gave His life to serve us, we give our lives to serve each other. And because He rose from the dead, our service will be effective.

Maybe you've tried to invest in someone else. You've tried to come alongside them and help them follow Jesus, and it didn't go well. Or maybe you've never tried because you don't think you can do it. You've heard sermons on this topic and thought, *I don't know enough. No one would listen to me. It's not natural to me.* Those things may be true, but they're irrelevant. Making disciples is not about your intelligence, eloquence, or impressiveness but the victorious Jesus working through you to impact someone else's life. It's a divine calling, empowered by divine grace.

Imagine visiting a friend's house, and it's garbage night. You pull in and see his garbage cans out at the curb. Leaning next to one is a brand-new, unused, expensive vacuum cleaner. You go inside and ask him about it. He tells you he wanted to clean his floors, so he bought the best, but no matter how many times he vacuumed the floors, they never got clean. He would go over and over them, but nothing would happen. He vacuumed every night for weeks, and his floors kept getting dirtier. His experience seems strange to you, so you ask him to walk you through what he did. He describes coming home from the store, pulling the vacuum cleaner out of the box, assembling it, flipping the "ON" switch, and pushing it around the house, but nothing happened. All of a sudden, it dawns on you, and you ask the million-dollar question, the question that clears everything up. You ask him, "Did you plug it in?"

Without power, your mightiest effort will accomplish nothing. Without the empowering grace of Jesus Christ, your attempts to impact other church members will only fail. We think we need to be smarter, work harder, be more educated, get more support, have a track record of success, or have the right circumstances. None of those things determine the impact we have on others. What matters is whether we're trying to disciple people in our strength or relying on the grace of Jesus.

Conclusion

Paul discipled Timothy and commanded Timothy to disciple others. Those others were to disciple others. This is the grand scheme for the advancement of Christianity. Because it is empowered by Jesus, it has been effective. For 2,000 years, the church has embraced this pattern of discipleship. Individual Christians fully committed and engaged in serving Jesus, investing their lives in other people's lives for their own good and the glory of Jesus Christ.

What does this kind of discipleship look like in a healthy church today? A church filled with members committed to making disciples will function like a teaching hospital. They are first a hospital where sick, hurting, and broken people can come to find healing. The church isn't perfect, but Jesus is, and there is no sickness He can't heal. So the members spread their arms wide open and invite everyone to come, meet Jesus, and be made brand-new.

But this kind of church isn't just a hospital. It's committed to being a teaching hospital. It longs to help the hurting but also to produce doctors. This church wants to see men and women be trained inside its walls and go out and start new hospitals around the world. Hospitals in another city or another state. Hospitals in places the name of Jesus has never been spoken. This church takes training seriously, investing in church planters and cross-cultural missionaries, who will learn from the pastors and prepare for a future of ministry. They will commit time and money to train spiritual physicians to take the remedy to those infected by sin.

You may hear that and think that's a beautiful goal for a church. You may encourage your pastors to do that, patting them on the back: "Great job, guys. Keep up the good work. Train some more doctors." Don't you realize that hospitals need more than just doctors? A hospital that only employed doctors wouldn't stay in business long. The hospital needs nurses, technicians, clerks, cooks, guards, and janitors. Without them, the doctors would quickly be ineffective.

So maybe you're not a doctor, you're "just" a janitor in this spiritual hospital. Just a guard, just a clerk. Every position is important. Every member matters. Whatever your role, you need to train someone else. Just as we need future doctors, we need future clerks, future nurses, and future cooks. A healthy church doesn't just produce doctors, they build other hospitals. And that will only happen as each church member trains others, as committed disciples train new disciples.

Chapter Six

Every Member a Giver

The elder: To my dear friend Gaius, whom I love in the truth. Dear friend, I pray that you are prospering in every way and are in good health, just as your whole life is going well. For I was very glad when fellow believers came and testified to your fidelity to the truth—how you are walking in truth. I have no greater joy than this: to hear that my children are walking in truth. Dear friend, you are acting faithfully in whatever you do for the brothers and sisters, especially when they are strangers. They have testified to your love before the church. You will do well to send them on their journey in a manner worthy of God, since they set out for the sake of the Name, accepting nothing from pagans. Therefore, we ought to support such people so that we can be coworkers with the truth.

3 John 1:1–8

Giving is one of those topics that makes people feel uncomfortable. There are reasons we're uncomfortable with this topic. One reason is that we all struggle with selfishness. It's easy to be selfish with our time, energy, and of course, our money. So, the topic of giving is one that we know will probably expose some level of selfishness in us. Another reason is because of skepticism about churches and money. There are high-profile stories of churches wasting money on luxuries, pastors living in mansions, and traveling evangelists with private jets. These abuses have colored the way many people think about money and "organized religion."

In the mid-1980s, a sincere, trained pastor believed God called him and his family to serve as foreign missionaries. They met with a missions organization and shared their desire to go to some small islands in the Pacific to share the gospel with a people group that had few encounters with Christianity. Due to some unrest in those islands, the missions organization asked them to consider serving as missionaries on different Pacific islands—the Hawaiian islands. You can imagine how some of their conversations went. People would joke with him all the time, "I wish God would call me to Hawaii to serve there." Despite being qualified for the role and demonstrating the significant need for gospel missionaries to go, he was never able to raise the money necessary to serve there. People were skeptical, and their skepticism kept them from giving.

We understand why people are skeptical. Sensitivity to skepticism often keeps otherwise healthy churches from addressing the topic of giving. They may not consciously avoid it but certainly don't pursue it. But the topic of giving, of using our money for something more than our own needs and wishes, is too important to ignore. In fact, if you read the Gospel accounts closely, you'll find that Jesus often talks about money. Giving is a significant responsibility for every Christian. It is one of the vital roles each member plays in the church's ongoing mission. Members should give regularly, generously, and cheerfully to their local church.

The Message of Third John

The shortest book in the New Testament, 3 John, outlines four reasons each church member should also be a giver. Before we look at the reasons, allow us to summarize the message of this epistle. Third John is a letter written by the apostle John that focuses on three individuals.

The first individual, Gaius, is the recipient of the letter. John commends him for his faithfulness, especially in hosting and supporting Christian missionaries, and then encourages him to continue to do so. The second individual, Diotrephes, is causing problems in a nearby church because he refuses to listen to apostolic teaching. He loves to be in charge, so when missionaries come from the apostles, he refuses to receive them and even threatens anyone who shows them hospitality. The third individual, Demetrius, is likely the one who brought this letter to Gaius from John. John is assuring Gaius that Demetrius is a faithful brother who can be trusted.

This short letter encourages a Christian to remain faithful despite difficulty and opposition. From Gaius's example and John's instruction, we discover that giving is an important part of being a faithful church member.

Giving Indicates Your Level of Spiritual Health

> The elder: To my dear friend Gaius, whom I love in the truth. Dear friend, I pray that you are prospering in every way and are in good health, just as your whole life is going well. For I was very glad when fellow believers came

> and testified to your fidelity to the truth—how you are walking in truth. I have no greater joy than this: to hear that my children are walking in truth. (3 John 1–4)

John makes two positive statements about Gaius's spiritual condition: his soul is doing well (v. 2), and he is walking in the truth (v. 3). What evidence does he give to back up these statements? Gaius gladly welcomed some Christian brothers into his life and, as we will see in the coming verses, supported them as they ministered (vv. 5, 8). His willingness to give was an indication of spiritual health. John called what Gaius did a "faithful thing" (v. 5 ESV). Generosity is a mark of faithfulness because it shows commitment to others and confidence in God's ability to provide for you. Gaius demonstrated faith in God by giving what God had given him to others to bless them.

Giving does not guarantee a person is spiritually healthy, but a failure to give is a sure indicator of someone's lack of spiritual health. Is there any reason not to give other than a failure to trust that God will provide for you? Failure to give can also indicate that you don't truly prioritize the most important eternal things. Surely, a failure to give is not about resources because giving does not require a person to be rich. Jesus's most famous example of giving is a widow who gave her last two pennies.[1] The apostle Paul commended the Christians in Macedonia who amid "extreme poverty" [had] "overflowed in a wealth of generosity" (2 Cor. 8:2 ESV). Giving is not limited by your resources but by your faith.

Faith and giving go hand in hand. This is true in both the Old and New Testaments. It's true in ancient Israel and the modern church. Giving generously indicates spiritual health because it demonstrates faith that God will provide for you. Your future is not in your hands. Why were the Israelites commanded to bring the first of their harvest to God? Did God need it? No, it wasn't for Him, but for them. They learned to trust Him by giving. Giving was a sign of their faith and a way to grow in faith.

If you struggle to give because you don't know if you'll make it, the most liberating and terrifying thing you can do is give. It's terrifying because you are placing your future outside your control, and it's liberating because your future is out of your control. Now, you're finally admitting it and entrusting yourself to God.

Surprisingly, we don't find a lot of commands to give in the New Testament. In the place of commands, we find examples and expectations. When Jesus taught about giving, He simply assumed His disciples would give. He said to them, "When you give" (Matt. 6:2 ESV).

Not only do we find this expectation, but we also find warnings about selfishness. In a haunting condemnation of those who only use their resources for themselves, James writes: "You have lived luxuriously on the earth and have indulged yourselves. You have fattened your hearts in a day of slaughter" (James 5:5). Spending all your money on yourself is like a steer eating extra helpings of feed on the way to the slaughterhouse. It's not just a warning; it's also an observation. A sign of spiritual sickness is selfishness.

Giving is part of being spiritually healthy. Growing in giving is part of becoming a more mature follower of Jesus. Paul encourages believers to "excel in everything" (2 Cor. 8:7)—in faith, speech, knowledge, earnestness, love, and giving. Now, it is possible to be spiritually weak, even spiritually dead, and still give. Famously, Ananias and Sapphira gave a large gift and ended up dead due to deceitful hearts.[2] So, giving does not guarantee spiritual health, but it is one indication of it.

We want you to be spiritually healthy. One of the reasons every church member should give is because every church member should be growing in faith. Your pastors want to be able to say about you that your soul "is doing well," "that you are walking in the truth," and "that you are filled with faith." These statements will not be possible if you use money selfishly, if you never grow into a generous, sacrificial, and consistent giver.

Giving Clarifies What You Love

> Dear friend, you are acting faithfully in whatever you do for the brothers and sisters, especially when they are strangers. They have testified to your love before the church. (3 John 5–6a)

Why did Gaius open his home, heart, and wallet to these traveling preachers? It wasn't because they were his friends. He didn't even know them. They were strangers.[3] The reason was love. Gaius loved God and God's people more than he loved his own money.

What do you love? These other Christians testified to his love because they had seen him spend his money to help them. What testimony would be given about your love? How we spend or save our money is a sign of what we love. Jesus clarified this when He said: "For where your treasure is, there your heart will be also" (Matt. 6:21). Your heart and your wallet are best friends. What you spend money on reveals what you love.

When Paul encouraged the Christians in Corinth to give generously to help another church in need, he said their giving would prove that their love was "genuine" (2 Cor. 8:8 ESV). Saying they loved this other church and saying they would pray for this church would not prove their love. Sending this church some hard-earned cash would demonstrate that they did indeed love them.

Because giving is so closely tied to what we love, it has always been a part of the worship gathering of God's people. We worship what we love and live for, so when we gather with God's people to worship Him, we say we love and live for God. One of the ways we say this is by giving as part of our worship. This was evident when the Israelites came to the temple to worship. They would come bearing sacrifices, both crops and livestock. They didn't show up to worship God empty-handed. These gifts were not attempts to earn God's blessing but an expression of worship to God. It was a way of showing that God was more important and loved than anything else in their life. They gave God their best from a heart of love as an act of worship.

When the church gathered in the New Testament, they gave as part of their worship. They gave to help those in need,[4] they pooled money to send to other churches,[5] and they supported gospel work[6] and gospel workers.[7] Even here, the context is a man involved in a local church, giving to help spread the gospel, and the report of his giving is shared with a local church. Three times, the church is mentioned in this short letter.[8]

Think about what you do when you gather with your church each Sunday. You gather together to worship. You wake up, get dressed, and gather because you love God. You display your love for God by taking the time to meet together. You also do it by caring for each other before, during, and after the service. You sing about your love for God and listen to what He says in His Word. If you do all of this, but no one ever mentions money, no one never mentions giving, what does that say about our love for Him? Could it legitimately be called into question?

Imagine an extended family gathering at Christmastime. One of the nieces brings a boyfriend with her. You start talking to them, and they say they are so in love. They hold hands and give each other silly in-love looks. He tells her how beautiful she is, and everyone "oohs and ahs." They talk about marriage and how much they mean to each other. When it comes time to give gifts, she hands him a beautifully wrapped Christmas present, and inside is the perfect gift. It's not only expensive, but it's extremely thoughtful. Now it's his turn. He shrugs and says, "I didn't get her anything." What would you think? He said he loved her. He told her she looked beautiful. He held her hand and looked at her like he was in love. Wouldn't that be enough? Absolutely not! If he loved her, he would demonstrate that love by giving her something of value. Is it so different between us and God? What we spend our money on clarifies what we love.

We see a negative example of this in Diotrephes, who loves himself.[9] Is it any surprise that he is unwilling to be hospitable, unwilling to receive other Christians, unwilling to support those who are ministering the gospel?[10] What you spend money on reveals what you love. Do you love Jesus? Do you love His people? Do you love the gospel? Do you want it to spread?

Giving Reveals Your Understanding of God's Grace

> You will do well to send them on their journey in a manner worthy of God. (3 John 6)

John commends Gaius for supporting these messengers and encourages him to do it again. Some others are coming and John wants Gaius to open his house once again and support them as they continue on their way. He uses a fascinating phrase to describe how Gaius should support them. He should support them "in a manner worthy of God"—support them in a way that fits the character of God. Give how God gives. How would Gaius know how God gives?

Because he's experienced it. He is a recipient of God's grace, and his understanding of God's grace will shape how he gives to others. "Give in a manner worthy of God" demands you understand how God gives. We know from Scripture that God gives sacrificially—He offered Himself for us. He gives abundantly—He desires to pour the riches of grace on us for all eternity. He gives cheerfully—this is obvious in His creative work and the promise of a new, greater creation. The way we give reveals how we think about the way God gives. What does your giving say about the way God gives? Or better, what does your giving say about the way you understand how God gives?

Giving and the gospel go hand in hand. The lengthiest section we have on giving in the New Testament is in 2 Corinthians 8–9. The apostle Paul encourages a church to give generously to assist other churches whose members are suffering due to persecution and drought. He encourages them by reminding them of the gospel, what God has done for us through Jesus Christ. Here is the heart of his encouragement: "For you know the grace of our Lord Jesus Christ: Though he was rich, for your sake he became poor, so that by his poverty you might become rich" (2 Cor. 8:9). This should be all the encouragement we need to give generously. Jesus, who was rich (what an understatement), became poor (another understatement), so we who are poor might become rich. You got that? Now give as He gave.

Laura often sends her husband heartwarming videos knowing he will not be able to watch them without crying. Over time, it has become a family game of sorts. Military reunion videos between a dad and his kids have a 100 percent success rate. As expected, her tender husband weeps like a baby. More often than not, their children watch the video as well and shed tears just like their father. Indeed, they resemble their father in how they respond to touching, heart-warming stories.

Your goal in giving should be to resemble your Father in how you give. Give just like He gives. Give so often and so much that someone could predict how you will respond when you hear about a need. They'll see your generosity and think, *He is just like his Father. She is just like her Father.*

Giving Engages You in the Mission of God

> Since they set out for the sake of the Name, accepting nothing from pagans. Therefore, we ought to support such people so that we can be coworkers with the truth. (3 John 7–8)

Gaius became a fellow worker with these missionaries by supporting their mission. Their mission was to spread Jesus's glory to people at home and abroad. Their motive to go was for the Name—the reputation of Jesus Christ. Christians are spreading the glory of Jesus locally and around the world, and we partner with them by giving. God has chosen to fund the spread of the gospel by giving Christians. He could do it another way, but He has chosen this way. God's people support God's work by giving back what God has given to them.

This instruction is given to the church. "The elders who are good leaders are to be considered worthy of double honor, especially those who work hard at preaching and teaching. For the Scripture says: Do not muzzle an ox while it is treading out the grain, and, 'The worker is worthy of his wages'" (1 Tim. 5:17–18). As a church member, you should financially support those laboring for the spread of the gospel in your local church and around the globe.

This is our responsibility. We ought to support gospel workers and gospel work.[11] The verb *ought* carries a sense of obligation. It's in the present tense, which means our continual obligation is to partner financially in gospel work. Supporting the gospel's spread with your gifts is not a preference but a responsibility.

If we don't do it, who will? We can't expect non-Christians to fund the spread of the gospel. These gospel workers would not accept money from the Gentiles (non-Christians). We shouldn't appeal to non-Christians to pay for the gospel because it undermines the message of free grace. If they paid for it, they might think their payment earned them the right to be saved. It would confuse them about what it means to be entirely undeserving of grace and still receive it because of God's overwhelming love.

God funds His mission with your gifts. Don't think that makes Him dependent on you as if He needs your help. He desires your participation in His work. God asking for your help is like Grandma asking you to bring a side dish to Thanksgiving dinner. She doesn't need it. She can do it better, but she wants you to be a part of it. God doesn't need us, but He invites us to participate in what He's doing.

The gospel moves forward through Christians giving regularly, generously, and cheerfully. When you become a member of a church, you probably made a couple of commitments that sounded something like this: "We will support the ministry of the church through our time, effort, and money. We will support through prayer and giving those whom the church sends to proclaim the gospel beyond our community."

We promise to support gospel work in our community and beyond with our money. We promise to engage in the mission of God. That's what you're doing when you give each week. You are funding the spread of the gospel. This is how we need to view our giving—not as a mere obligation, checkbox, or duty, but as an investment in people's lives and a propellant for gospel advancement. As one writer said, "To put our money where our mouth is shows the world our commitment to the gospel of Jesus Christ."[12]

Sometimes, it's easier to see how our giving propels the gospel when we give to foreign missions than when we give to our own church. The connection between the spread of the gospel and our giving is clear when we look at a couple living and working in a foreign country. Though it may not be quite as clear, all your giving to the church goes to gospel advancement.

Consider the money your church spends on its building, especially if you rent or are paying off a mortgage. It's probably a lot of money. Wouldn't that money be better spent on evangelism, discipleship, and missions? It *is* being spent on evangelism, discipleship, and missions. Just examine what happens on a Sunday morning in your church building because you and the other members give to pay for the space. In the auditorium, people will gather to worship Jesus and listen to His Word. In classrooms, children will be taught the gospel. In the hallways, Christians will encourage each other to faithfulness. Students and adults will be equipped to live out their faith in classes.

The gospel ministry on Sunday morning and the resulting ministry throughout the week all happen because your giving helps pay the rent. If you step back and look, I bet you can picture some foreign missionaries serving on the field forty years from now who trusted Christ in your church building one Sunday morning because you gave to help pay the mortgage. The local church is the hub of gospel work, and your giving to the church supports ongoing gospel ministry.

Application

As we have seen, giving changes us and changes the world. We give so the gospel can be offered to others free of charge. If we break down 1 Corinthians 16:2, we can find a few practical steps to grow as givers:

> On the first day of the week, each of you is to set something aside and save in keeping with how he is prospering, so that no collections will need to be made when I come.

First, make giving your first financial priority. "Each person" should "set something aside." That is, each person should plan and prioritize giving. In the Old Testament, giving was primarily done in a tithe, the first 10 percent. It was also done by offering the first fruits of a harvest. Giving was the top priority. Giving is much easier when you do it first and then figure out your other priorities afterward. If you do it last, you'll often just give God any leftovers that remain. Rather than asking, "What am I required to do?" We should ask, "How can I manage the resources God has given me so I can give more to advance His kingdom?" That is what it means to make giving your first priority.

Second, give every week. Again, Paul encouraged Christians to do this, "On the first day of the week" in "keeping with how he is prospering." This is a simple way to make giving a priority. Since giving is part of your worship of God, connect it to your weekly worship. And do so in a way that is proportionate to your income.

Do it first, and do it each week. Give generously in proportion to what God has given you. After all, we are stewards of what belongs to God. All that we give comes from His hand.[13] These simple steps will help you grow in faithfulness. This chapter could have been shorter. We could have written just one sentence: "Give because God commands it." Obedience should be reason enough to give. But God lists other reasons we should give. He shows us why we give. We give because giving is one of the ways we learn to trust Him. We give because it helps us love what matters. We give because we look most like our gracious Father and because He has invited us to be part of what He is doing around the world.

Conclusion

A giving Christian is one of the most powerful witnesses to the truth of the gospel. Lee Strobel, author of *A Case for Christ*, described the powerful impact one Christian's giving had on him before he was a Christian.[14] He was serving as a reporter for the *Chicago Tribune*, and he couldn't move past a story he wrote about the Delgado family as part of a series on Chicago's poorest citizens.

At the time Strobel met the Delgado family—Grandma Perfecta and her two grandchildren, Lydia and Jenny—he was not a Christian. But they were. In spite of their horrid living conditions, Perfecta couldn't stop talking about Jesus. Here she was living in abject poverty in a small vermin-infested apartment, yet she was not wallowing in despair but exuding hope in God's faithfulness.

As Christmas grew close, Strobel struggled to understand how Perfecta could be poor and happy while he was affluent but empty. On Christmas Eve he got in his car and went to visit them. What he found shocked him.

> When Jenny opened the door, I couldn't believe my eyes. *Tribune* readers had responded to my article by showering the Delgados with a treasure trove of gifts—roomfuls of furniture, appliances, and rugs; a lavish Christmas tree with piles of wrapped presents underneath; carton upon bulging carton of food; and a dazzling selection of clothing, including dozens of warm winter coats, scarves, and gloves. On top

> of that, they donated thousands of dollars in cash.
>
> But as surprised as I was by this outpouring, I was even more astonished by what my visit was interrupting: Perfecta and her granddaughters were getting ready to give away much of their newfound wealth. When I asked Perfecta why, she replied in halting English: "Our neighbors are still in need. We cannot have plenty while they have nothing. This is what Jesus would want us to do."

Strobel could not understand this type of generosity. It made no sense to him. How could they be so generous when they had so little? When he asked Perfecta how she could give away what others had given her, she responded with rich, deep, beautiful gospel truth. She told Lee she had done nothing to deserve it. Everything under the tree was God's gift to them, but none of it compared to His greatest gift. The gift they would celebrate the next morning. The gift of His Son, Jesus. Strobel was forever changed by the generosity he witnessed that night.

> To her, this child in the manger was the undeserved gift that meant everything—more than material possessions, more than comfort, more than security. And at that moment, something inside of me wanted desperately to know this Jesus—because, in a sense, I saw Him in Perfecta and her granddaughters.[15]

We give because Jesus gave everything for us. We give because Jesus is enough. And we give so that the good news of Jesus might be seen by those who don't know Him.

Chapter Seven

Every Member an Intercessor

I give thanks to my God for every remembrance of you, always praying with joy for all of you in my every prayer, because of your partnership in the gospel from the first day until now. I am sure of this, that he who started a good work in you will carry it on to completion until the day of Christ Jesus. Indeed, it is right for me to think this way about all of you, because I have you in my heart, and you are all partners with me in grace, both in my imprisonment and in the defense and confirmation of the gospel. For God is my witness, how deeply I miss all of you with the affection of Christ Jesus. And I pray this: that your love will keep on growing in knowledge and every kind of discernment, so that you may approve the things that are superior and may be pure and blameless in the day of Christ, filled with the fruit of righteousness that comes through Jesus Christ to the glory and praise of God.
Philippians 1:3–11

In medieval warfare, soldiers would line up in a shield wall. Those in the front rank would overlap their shields so there was no gap for a sword to penetrate. Those in the second rank would take their shields, tilt them, and place them over the heads of those in the front row. This would protect them from a spear or arrow. An army arrayed in a shield wall was hard to defeat, as long as each soldier kept their shield in the right spot.

In the famous passage on the armor of God, Christians are commanded to take up the shield of faith to quench the fiery arrows of the devil. The command to "take up" is plural, given to Christians as a group, not just to Christians individually. As each Christian takes up their shield, they not only protect themselves, but protect those around them. Your faith not only protects you from burning projectiles, but it protects those in close proximity to you. A solitary soldier with a shield can only protect one side, but a company in a shield wall can protect from attacks in all directions. You need others, and others need you, which is why joining a church is one of God's chief means of preserving His people.

Shortly after the command to take up the shield of faith, we find the command to pray constantly, not just for our own needs, but for other Christians. We are to make "intercession for all the saints" (Eph. 6:18). The context clarifies the saints as those Christians who are members of the same church.[1] As a member, you need to intercede regularly for the other members of your church. The church is a family of men and women set apart by God for His purpose—we are saints not because of what we've done, but because of what God has done for us. One way we care for each other is by praying by name for each other. We intercede on each other's behalf before the Father. We ask Him to help in times of difficulty. We shield each other from danger with faith-filled prayer.

We get a clear picture of intercessory prayer as the apostle Paul describes the way he prays for Christians located in the ancient city of Philippi.

Intercessory Prayer Rehearses God's Work

His prayer begins with gratitude to God for the work He's done in the lives of the Philippian Christians. God not only saved this group of Christians, but He brought them into a partnership with Paul that supported and sustained the work Paul was doing of taking the gospel to other places.

> I give thanks to my God for every remembrance of you, always praying with joy for all of you in my every prayer, because of your partnership in the gospel from the first day until now. (Phil. 1:3–5)

God made this group partakers of His grace,[2] and the outflow of grace is gospel partnership. Receiving the gospel of grace naturally leads people to partner together in the spread of the gospel of grace. This was true of this young church. God brought Paul to the city of Philippi, God brought people into Paul's path to hear the gospel, God saved those people, and God gathered them into a church. That church supported Paul, both in prayer and giving, as he went to a new city to preach the gospel again. Paul saw all of this as evidence of God's work in them.

Thinking about others, specifically about the evidence of God's work in their lives, energized Paul's prayer. If your prayer time lacks joy, then start here. Start by thanking God for the good work He's doing in the lives of the fellow members in your church. Your expressions of gratitude may be nothing more than short statements thanking God for His work in people's lives. If you've ever been part of a prayer meeting where Christians started to thank God for the good fruit He is producing in people's lives, you don't pay attention to the clock. You're too busy listening, reflecting, and thanking God to worry about what time it is.

Most of us don't get bored telling a story, especially us pastors. Give us a group of people, and we enjoy telling a good story. Our wives often remind us of how often we repeat the same stories. All it takes is someone to make a comment in a conversation that relates (even remotely) to one of our stories, and we are off like a field fire with a tailwind. Without question, our wives are somewhere in our vicinity, hanging their heads and sighing. They might get tired of hearing our stories, but we never tire of telling our stories. Tell God stories about the good things you see Him doing in the lives of those around you. Thank Him for the evidence of His grace you see in other people.

In order to do this, you need to know the other members of your church. The apostle Paul uses the same phrase four times in his prayer in Philippians 1 (ESV).

- Verse 4—"every prayer of mine for you all"
- Verse 7—"feel this way about you all"
- Verse 7—"you all are partakers"
- Verse 8—"I yearn for you all"

Paul didn't just love this church in general; he loved the individuals who made up this church, all of them. He invested in each of them. He prayed for each of them. He thanked God for each of them. And the more of them he knew and the more he knew about each of them, the more things he could thank God for.

If you want to be an intercessor, you need to invest in more relationships in your church, and you need to invest in deeper relationships. You should make it a goal to know as many people as possible at your church and learn how God is working in them.

Maybe you're thinking, *There's too many people. I can't possibly get to know every person.* How do you know? Have you tried? Have you made it a goal and failed? It may be impossible, but you'll never know until you actually try. "There's too many people" is a lazy excuse. It's something we say to make ourselves feel better for not trying.

The way to get to know more people, to hear their stories, to see God working in them is to start small. Start with your small group. Start with the people who volunteer in the same children's class or on the same ushering team. One by one invite them out for lunch or over for dinner. Ask them their story. Find out how God is working in their life. Write it down. The next time you pray, pull your notes out and tell God about your conversation with that person. Thank God for saving them and for continuing to work in their life.

Not only will this energize your praying, but it will also protect you from a critical spirit. It's interesting to see how Paul told each church he was thankful for them, even the church in the city of Corinth. That church was messed up. In spite of their mess, Paul still saw evidence of God's grace in them. Thanking God energizes prayer while killing pride.

Tony Merida and Francis Chan give this advice:

> If you're a super-critical person, always focusing on what's wrong, then you won't be a grateful person. Don't look for perfection before you show gratitude; look for evidences of grace in people's lives. Be quick to thank God for Christian virtues in others, and remember that sanctification is a slow process.[3]

"Be quick to thank God for Christian virtues in others"—that's great counsel. Start your time of prayer by thinking about faces you see on Sunday and thanking God for what you see Him doing in their lives. Intercessory prayer rehearses God's work.

And rehearsing God's work will bring you joy as you pray. Imagine if you went on a date like we often pray. First of all, that date might end up being very short. By the time your car pulled out of the driveway, the date would be over. Sometimes you may not even have time to start the car to go on the date before you're done. But on this particular day, you set aside time to pray. If your date looked like your time of prayer, your date might not be thrilled with how often you yawned and nodded off during the date. Or how easily distracted you were—the number of times you quick-checked an email and responded partway through a sentence.

But maybe it's a day that you are really focused. A day you are devoted to a significant time of prayer. What would your date think if you pulled out a long list of names, and started reading through them, saying somewhat generic things about each one? "The Millers—their dog is old and their grandma is sick, or maybe the other way around." "Now I'm telling you about the

Johnsons—they're really busy, bless them." After working your way through the entire list, you end, breathe a sigh of relief, and announce the date is done. You even walk away from the date pleased with yourself that you have done your duty. You have faithfully made it through the entire thing and haven't even fallen asleep once. You don't have to be an experienced dater to know that your date wouldn't feel honored and appreciated by your robotic performance of duty. You honor your date when you love them enough to enjoy the date. When a date with them brings you delight, it makes them feel loved.

Prayer, like a date, is a conversation between two people who love each other; yet so often it feels like a chore. As the apostle Paul introduces this letter to the church in Philippians, he tells them he prays regularly for them, and he says he makes his "prayer with joy." Praying with joy. Would you describe your times of prayer as joyful? We generally place prayer in the column marked *duty*, not the column marked *delight*. But it doesn't need to be this way. It shouldn't be this way. Prayer can, and should, be marked by joy.

What does joyful prayer look like? Our first thought may be that it's prayer in good times, but this letter was written from prison. Paul was chained to a Roman soldier. Joy in prayer is not dependent on circumstances. Joy comes as you remember and rehearse all the ways you see God working in the lives of those you love.

Intercessory Prayer Trusts Future Grace

The apostle Paul not only rehearses evidence of God's past work in the lives of the believers in Philippi, but he also looks ahead with confidence to what God will do in the future.

> I am sure of this, that he who started a good work in you will carry it on to completion until the day of Christ Jesus. (Phil. 1:6)

Often when we pray for people, we're praying for them in times of need. Maybe the need is a health problem, a relationship problem, or a financial problem. We don't know how it will turn out, and so we pray with uncertainty. Paul's prayers focus primarily on the ongoing effects of the gospel in people's lives, and so he prays with a high level of certainty and confidence. He knows that when God calls a person to Himself, He will keep that person to the end, no matter what circumstances they face. This confidence is clear in Paul's letter to the Romans.

> For those he foreknew he also predestined to be conformed to the image of his Son, so that he would be the firstborn among many brothers and sisters. And those he predestined, he also called; and those he called, he also justified; and those he justified, he also glorified. (Rom. 8:29–30)

The grace that saves a person will sustain that person until the end. When you pray by rehearsing evidence of God's grace in people's lives, your prayer will naturally raise a question. Will His work continue? Will the good things God is doing in them persist? If you are uncertain, then it will be hard to pray with confidence or joy. Your joy in prayer will be replaced by a growing sense of anxiety, even dread. But joyful prayer continues because of confidence that the grace we see now will not somehow expire in the future.

One of the great joys in the Christian life is reuniting with people who have invested in our spiritual lives. There have been times when we have returned to the churches we grew up in and seen the nursery workers who prayed over us as they rocked us to sleep. We've run into the teachers who prayed for our spiritual growth as teenagers and even former pastors who have prayed for us throughout our ministries. Those meetings are often full of joy, hugs, and sometimes tears. They are reminders that God uses people—and their prayers—to shape us into the people we have become.

One of God's sweet gifts to the church is to see people endure in faith over decades. When we pray for each other, we can do so confidently, knowing that God will never give up on His children. Confidence in future grace is what nourishes a life of faith. Jesus knows this. He created us this way, and it's why He attaches promises to commands. He tells us to go into the world and make disciples, and then promises the grace necessary to sustain obedience—"And remember, I am with you always (Matt. 28:18–20). We can never outpace grace. No matter how far we go or how long we travel, grace is our constant companion. Your tank may run dry, but God's grace is never exhausted.

Our confidence needs to be in God's grace and not in our own performance. We can't help but contrast what Paul says to these Christians in Philippi with what he said to a group of Christians in Galatia. To the Philippians he says, "God will complete what He began." To the Galatians he asks, "Why are you trying to complete by works what God began in you through faith?" (see Gal. 3:1–4). The key to endurance is trusting the grace of God. It's to remind ourselves daily that our standing before God is fixed. Our identity in Christ is unchanging.

The God who promised to restore His creation will fully restore His people. And the day Christ returns will be a day of joy the likes of which we can hardly imagine. For this reason we intercede for other members of the church with confidence that God will complete His good work in them.

Intercessory Prayer Nourishes Deep Affections

We can feel the love Paul has for these saints throughout this prayer, but he mentions it specifically in Philippians 1:7–8.

> Indeed, it is right for me to think this way about all of you, because I have you in my heart, and you are all partners with me in grace, both in my imprisonment and in the defense and confirmation of the gospel. For God is my witness, how deeply I miss all of you with the affection of Christ Jesus.

See how strongly the apostle loves this group of Christians. He "yearns" to be with them. The word *yearns* evokes a dog straining at a leash, eager to run. It brings to mind a child at the airport waiting for a parent to return, being held back at security. He desperately wants to be with them. So he clearly loves this group of Christians. But here is a question for you to consider.

Does he pray for them because he loves them, or does he love them because he prays for them?

We can't pick one or the other. Prayer both reveals and shapes our affections. He prays for them because he loves them, and he loves them even more because he regularly prays for them. Joyful prayer deals with what we care most deeply about, and it also shapes what we care most deeply about. He cares deeply about these Christians, and he prays for them. His love and prayer are intertwined and indivisible.

The reason he loves them so much is not because he's an inherently compassionate person. His affection for them comes from Jesus,[4] and it's because they're partakers with him of grace.[5] This isn't natural affection, but the fruit of Jesus at work in Paul's heart. They had certainly gone through some challenging times together—they'd been with Paul when he was imprisoned for the gospel. They'd been at his side when he had to defend the gospel against attacks. So this affection was deepened by walking through difficulty together, but shared experience is not the ground of his affection for them.

The ground of his affection is union with Jesus Christ. They have each experienced the transforming grace of Jesus—they have met Jesus and been changed. Their lives are different because they have been immersed in the overwhelming, extravagant mercy of God. Paul deeply loves these Christians, and so he prays for them. When you're praying for someone you really care about, prayer won't be a drudgery.

Here are two statements that at first may sound the same, but are more like two sides of the same coin:

- If you love people, you will talk to God about them. Prayer is a sign of love. True love motivates prayer.
- If you want to love people, start to talk to God about them. Prayer is not only a sign of love, but a spark for love. If you're struggling to love someone, begin praying for them. Begin talking to God about why you don't love them, but why you want to. Rehearse any evidence of grace you see in them. Pray for them to grow and flourish. If you begin praying for someone, God will help you grow to love them.

We're most animated when we talk about what we love. Prayer that's honest with God about what you love will never be boring. It will never be dull. Intercessory prayer for the brothers and sisters in your church nourishes deep affections.

Intercessory Prayer Anticipates Spiritual Growth

He ends the prayer with requests for them to grow, and he makes these requests with confidence. He's already told them God will work in them to complete them. These requests reveal what God is doing and will continue to do in these believers.

> And I pray this: that your love will keep on growing in knowledge and every kind of discernment, so that you may approve the things that are superior and may be pure and blameless in the day of Christ, filled with the fruit of

> righteousness that comes through Jesus Christ
> to the glory and praise of God. (Phil. 1:9–10)

His prayer anticipates that the Philippian Christians will grow more loving—their love will abound more and more. Love for whom? For God? For each other? For the nations? Yes, all of the above. The love God pours into His people is not confined to a select group, but overflows in love for all people.

What does love abounding more and more look like? As God answers this prayer, how will it be evident in the lives of these Christians? They'll give more and more of themselves to each other. They won't be stingy with their time, energy, money, or affection. They'll grow more and more selfless—putting one another's needs before their own. They won't be petty and mean-spirited, but generous and patient.

He prays for their love to "abound more and more"—he doesn't ask for them to have a little more love or a touch more love. He asks for it to abound, expand, overflow, and to do so over and over. He asks for God to do something big in their hearts. When you pray, don't set your sights low. Aim high. Pray for things money can't buy and people can't accomplish. Pray for things that require God to do the impossible.

When a Christian prays for a church, it's tempting to pray for physical needs. For instance, if a pastor is leading his church through a building campaign it's easy to focus his attention primarily on a new building, especially for the money necessary to build. It's okay to pray for God to provide a building, but our first request should be that God would change the hearts of the people to become more generous. The pastor should pray for each member to increase in faith, for God to do a work in and through the members that defies human explanation. He should pray with confidence that God will answer his prayer because God promises to work in the lives of His people.

The Beatles released a song in 1967 called "All You Need Is Love." The song, though catchy, was wrong then, just as it's wrong now. You need more than love, and we see that in Paul's prayer. He wants them to grow in love, but he knows that love is not enough. He wants their love[6] to come with increased knowledge and discernment so they will approve what's excellent.[7] Like The Beatles, our culture is confused about the nature of love. We're told love accepts whatever another person says. Love affirms whatever another person feels. But that's not real love. Real love seeks what's best for others, even if they don't see it.

We know this is true in parenting. Real love doesn't allow kids to do whatever they want to do. Little kids want to do lots of stupid things. Little kids put dangerous things in their mouths, run out in the street, touch hot stoves, stick things in outlets, and on and on. Love doesn't say, "That's fine, sweetie. Do whatever you feel like." Love seeks what's best for them, even if they don't like it.

The reason Paul prays for their love to grow in discernment is because he knows how much help we need to love others well.

- You know you should love your spouse, but do you always know how to best love your spouse?
- You know you should love your kids, but do you know how to love them when

they're rebellious and seem to want nothing to do with you?
- You know you should love your neighbor, but do you know how to love that cranky neighbor who keeps getting angry at you for no reason?

We need supernatural insight to know how best to love people when it's difficult. Discerning love helps us "approve what is excellent." That's our goal. We want to love others with such insight that we point them to what's excellent. We help them see and understand what's best. This is why Bible study, discipleship, and teaching are such an important part of the church's life together. Constant exposure to God's Word sharpens our spiritual senses, so that we perceive what is excellent. A lone sermon doesn't make us discerning, but the combined weight of months, years, decades of Scripture equips us with wisdom and insight.

Spiritual growth has two goals: the return of Christ and the glory of God.[8] The more we grow, the more prepared we are for the return of Christ. We're becoming more like Jesus, filled with the fruit of His righteousness. And the more we grow, the more people will see the glory of God on display in us. Our growth in Christ will be evident to all, and it will come as we pray for those who worship alongside us each week. When you intercede for the other members of your church, you should ask for and expect spiritual growth.

Conclusion

Too often prayer and joy seem at odds. They appear to be mortal enemies rather than best friends. This passage shows us how prayer and joy work together. We can enjoy prayer, and prayer can fuel our joy.

There are two things in life that always kill joy—selfishness and shallowness. Intercessory prayer eliminates these two joy-killers. We can't thank God for the growth of others and pray for their continued growth while still being selfish, and we can't expose our deepest affections while remaining shallow. Prayer produces joy when it causes us to look out for others and dig deep into our own hearts to discover what we really care about.

Think about the kinds of stories we most love. They're not stories of selfishness and shallowness. Their stories of someone laying down his life to save someone else. Stories of a group of people coming together for something bigger than their individual lives.

- In *The Lion King*, Simba starts off as selfish and shallow. What if he never changed?
- What if Robin Hood stole from the rich, but kept it for himself so he could buy more stuff?
- What if the princess was kidnapped and guarded by the dragon, but none of the knights would go rescue her because they were too busy playing video games?

Stories of selfishness and shallowness are a waste of time. No one wants to hear them. But stories of transformation, growth, sacrifice, and love—these are the stories we enjoy. These are the stories that excite us, that delight us. Let these stories—real stories of God's transforming and sustaining grace in the lives of people around you—let them energize your praying. Learn them, tell them to God, and watch your joy in prayer increase as you intercede for the other members of your church.

Chapter Eight

Every Member an Ambassador

From now on, then, we do not know anyone from a worldly perspective. Even if we have known Christ from a worldly perspective, yet now we no longer know him in this way. Therefore, if anyone is in Christ, he is a new creation; the old has passed away, and see, the new has come! Everything is from God, who has reconciled us to himself through Christ and has given us the ministry of reconciliation. That is, in Christ, God was reconciling the world to himself, not counting their trespasses against them, and he has committed the message of reconciliation to us. Therefore, we are ambassadors for Christ, since God is making his appeal through us. We plead on Christ's behalf, "Be reconciled to God." He made the one who did not know sin to be sin for us, so that in him we might become the righteousness of God.
2 Corinthians 5:16–21

Bruce stood before a group of friends and family members and told a heartwarming story of reconciliation. Thirty years earlier, Bruce's dad had left his wife to live with another woman. His betrayal had split the family in two. Bruce, his two sisters, and his mom were no longer a part of his dad's life. They were estranged. For three decades there was little contact, little relationship apart from a periodic birthday card.

But when Bruce heard that his dad's long-time girlfriend was diagnosed with cancer, he reached out. Slowly a relationship began to grow, and when Bruce and his two sisters attended the funeral of his father's girlfriend, true reconciliation began. Though the process of reconciliation included painful moments and conversations, it continued until his father's death.

When Bruce stood at his father's funeral and told the story of reconciliation, he explained how it was only the gospel of Jesus Christ that made it possible. The truth that Bruce, his mother, and his sisters had all been forgiven by God is what empowered them to forgive their father for his sins against the family. At that funeral, Bruce shared how reconciliation with God is at the heart of the gospel message.

You see, Bruce understands his Bible. He understands the foundational truths that shape our world, our outlook, and our future. Because of our sin, we are estranged from God, but God made a way for us to be reconciled to Him through the work of Jesus Christ on the cross. Reconciliation with God changes everything.

- It changes how we handle heartbreak and betrayal.
- It changes how we view other people.
- It changes how we understand the future that awaits us.
- It changes how we forgive and seek forgiveness.
- It changes how we value things in life.

Nothing remains the same if we've been reconciled to God. Reconciliation with God produces a seismic shift and the shock waves touch every part of our lives.

And reconciliation with God is the heartbeat of a gospel-grounded church. Every beat of the church's heart should pulse with reconciliation. Reconciliation is not something the church keeps near us, but something that flows through us. It's not right at our fingertips, it's streaming through our veins. We do not understand the cross of Jesus Christ, and we cannot be shaped by the cross, unless we understand how the cross reconciles us to God.

Bruce understood the urgent need for reconciliation, and he recognized that as a Christian he had been appointed as an ambassador of reconciliation. His king had commissioned him to speak on his behalf, and he was responsible to declare the king's message with clarity and boldness. Bruce didn't speak at the funeral because he's a paid minister. He's not. He's a retired math teacher who doesn't enjoy public speaking. He spoke because he takes his role as an ambassador seriously. Every member of the church has received the same commission. Each one of us has been appointed to represent King Jesus and share His news with the world around us.

Before we look at what an ambassador does, we need to make sure we understand the message of reconciliation. We can't fulfill our commission without being crystal clear on the message we're instructed to deliver, a message of reconciliation with God.

The Need for Reconciliation

> That is, in Christ, God was reconciling the world to himself, not counting their trespasses against them, and he has committed the message of reconciliation to us. (2 Cor. 5:19)

We need to be reconciled with God because we have trespassed something, and this trespass is counted against us. What have we trespassed? This question sends us back to the very beginning, when God first created mankind and placed them in the garden of Eden. He gave them everything they needed, not just to survive but to thrive. The world was theirs to cultivate and enjoy. But God gave them one inviolable law—they were not to eat of a certain tree in the middle of the garden.

This one law was for their good, and God's command was clear. But in a moment of temptation, they were not content to stay within the joy-filled protective confines of God's law, and they brazenly stepped over it, disregarding the boundary He established for their protection. In that moment of foolishness, their trespass brought deadly consequences. They were banished from the garden, and they were alienated from God. Their disregard for His authority and His command brought division and estrangement.

From that point forward, human history is a bit like the Netflix setting that starts playing another episode as soon as the current one ends. Adam and Eve violate God's command. Next episode: Cain kills Abel. A few episodes later: The whole earth is so corrupt that God sends a flood to judge humanity for their unbridled rebellion. As you flip through the pages of the Old Testament, you find episode after episode, and they each end the same way. Humanity trespassing God's law. The apostle Paul summarizes this teaching from the Old Testament in the letter he writes to the Romans. You can think of this like the recap at the start of a new episode. He basically begins with, "Previously in world history . . ." In chapter 1, he shows how non-Jews, with their disregard and ignorance of God, have trespassed God's law. Then in chapter 2, he focuses on the Jewish people and shows how they too have trespassed God's law, even while they immersed themselves in it. His famous conclusion in chapter 3 quotes from the Old Testament:

> For we have already charged that both Jews and Greeks are all under sin, as it is written: There is no one righteous, not even one. There is no one who understands; there is no one who seeks God. All have turned away; all alike have become worthless. There is no one who does what is good, not even one. (Rom. 3:9b–12)

Every single one of us has trespassed God's law. We have ignored the boundaries He set up for our good and rebelled against His authority over us. Our actions have cut us off from Him. This is important for us to understand. God did nothing to cause our estrangement. He didn't fail us in any way. He didn't break a promise or act in bad faith. God only did good. The responsibility for our estrangement from God falls completely on us.

Do you realize that your actions, your choices, your desires have cut you off from God? You will never truly understand the Christian message until you understand you are liable for your rebellion. God's law is summarized with two commands: love God with all your heart and love your neighbor as yourself. If you look at the record of your life, you will find repeated violations of both commands. Reconciliation with God is necessary because each of us stands guilty before God for our sinful disregard of His law.

The Process of Reconciliation

> Everything is from God, who has reconciled us to himself through Christ and has given us the ministry of reconciliation. That is, in Christ, God was reconciling the world to himself, not counting their trespasses against them, and he has committed the message of reconciliation to us. (2 Cor. 5:18–19)

How does reconciliation with God happen? Reconciliation begins with God taking the initiative. The one who was sinned against, whose law was violated makes the first move. He pursues the offending party (us), and He begins the work of reconciliation. Imagine if you robbed a bank, jumped into your getaway car, and fled the scene. The police begin to chase you, and you violate every traffic law trying to escape. When your car finally can't go any farther, the officer approaches your open window and says, "Do you know why I pulled you over?" You think, *It could be for speeding, running red lights, driving recklessly, resisting arrest, and robbing a bank.* But before you answer he says, "I pulled you over because the bank owner wanted you to know you're forgiven. He won't press charges."

God pursues rebels with grace. He chases after lawbreakers with mercy. But He doesn't ignore our trespasses. He doesn't pretend injustice never happened. He deals with our lawbreaking in a permanent, miraculous way.

> He made the one who did not know sin to be sin for us, so that in him we might become the righteousness of God. (2 Cor. 5:21)

In what is often called "The Great Exchange," Jesus took our sin (with all of its consequences) on Himself, and He gives us the righteousness that belongs to Him. This is what happened at the cross. Jesus, the perfect, sinless Son of God, became sin so that we might become righteous. Everything that rightly belonged to us—sin, judgment, condemnation, death—He took on Himself, so that everything that belonged to Him—righteousness, acceptance, pardon, life—could be given to us.

Notice that we don't just look righteous, but we become righteous.[1] Righteousness is not an activity we perform, but a state of being. It's the difference between an actress pretending to be married in a movie, and the same woman actually getting married in real life. When she recites those vows, her state of being changes. She becomes married, she doesn't just look married or identify as being married. She becomes married.

In a miraculous, mind-blowing way, when Jesus went to the cross, He became sin. Our sin was placed on Him in such a way that God could judge our sin—past, present, and future—fully and decisively in one ultimate act of judgment. At the very same time, the righteousness of God was given to us to such a degree that we have become righteous. Even though we still sin, we are no longer defined by our sin. When we sin now, it stands in contrast to who we are. It's unnatural for us as Christians to sin. We have been made righteous by the work of Jesus Christ on the cross.

John Piper powerfully summarizes reconciliation with God through Jesus: "When the Son of God died for our sins, he absorbed into himself, as he died, all the enmity that God had against his people. So the death of Christ is the objective, historical, unchangeable, rock-solid foundation of our reconciliation with God."[2]

Notice what's missing from reconciliation. Anything we do. Anything we offer. Anything we accomplish. We are reconciled to God "through Christ" (2 Cor. 5:18), not through good works, not through religious zeal, not through keeping the Ten Commandments, not through trying harder, not through getting baptized, not through going to church, not through being a good person. Reconciliation with God comes only through Jesus Christ.

Our only responsibility is to receive the grace He offers.[3] Reconciliation is a gift that must be accepted. God does all the work, and He offers it to us free of charge. But we must accept it. Accepting it requires us to acknowledge our guilt before Him and to admit that we need Him to fix what our actions have broken. We accept His forgiveness in faith, trusting that the work of Jesus is sufficient to cover our sin. Have you accepted the grace God offers through Jesus? Have you been reconciled with God?

Why do we need to be reconciled with God? Because we have violated His law. How does reconciliation with God happen? Through Jesus Christ alone.

The Effects of Reconciliation

> From now on, then, we do not know anyone from a worldly perspective. Even if we have known Christ from a worldly perspective, yet now we no longer know him in this way. Therefore, if anyone is in Christ, he is a new creation; the old has passed away, and see, the new has come! (2 Cor. 5:16–17)

The righteousness of God has changed us from the inside out, and we are brand-new. We are a new creation. We have been raised from the dead with Jesus to walk in newness of life. Everything is new, including the way we view people. That's Paul's point in verse 16. We don't see or judge people the same way now as we did before we were reconciled with God. In the past, we evaluated people from a worldly perspective. We were the same as all the other *American Idol* judges, evaluating people by how they looked, how they sounded, and what we thought they could accomplish. Our view of beauty was shaped by the culture, and so we idolized people who had a certain image, whether glamorous or powerful.

We evaluated people the same way Paul and his fellow Pharisees evaluated Jesus. At first they judged him as a good teacher, but over time they grew to dislike Him because He didn't affirm their way of doing things. So many people in that time viewed Jesus from a worldly perspective. They asked how He might benefit their lives and increase their comfort. Would He rescue them from Roman oppression? Would He make them feel superior to the Gentiles? They compared Him with other teachers and evaluated Him that way.

But those of us who have been reconciled with God see Jesus differently. We see Him for who He truly is. We see His glory and are awed by His grace. We are learning more and more about His compassion and care, His power and beauty, His joy and gladness. We don't see Him as a good teacher or good example, but as God. Worthy of our love and worthy of our lives. We see differently. Like Copernicus, who first realized the sun is at the center of the solar system, we realize that Jesus is at the very center of all things. Our lives are made to revolve around Him, not the other way around.

Not only is our way of seeing new, but everything is new. We are a new creation. We have new eyes to see Jesus, a new heart to love Him and others, a new nature of righteousness, a new identity as sons of God, a new destiny with God in a new heaven and new earth, we have new desires to please Him instead of ourselves, a new family of brothers and sisters, and a new purpose for life. We speak in a new way, think in a new way, and act in a new way. When God reconciles Himself to us, we don't turn over a new leaf. It's more like we're a part of a new forest sprouting in what used to be a desert.

The new has come, and the old has passed away. Do you realize that? If you're a Christian, you no longer need to be stuck in old ways of living. You are no longer imprisoned by past mistakes. Your failures don't define you. Do you believe that? So many of us struggle to move on from sins in our past. We still feel the shame that comes from sinful decisions, and we can't seem to shake it. Maybe deep down, we don't feel worthy enough to shake it. We think we deserve those feelings of shame as penance for the choices we made. But if God doesn't define us by our past sin, and if Jesus died for those sins, is it right for us to hold onto them? To hold onto our guilt?

If your sin was paid for by Jesus on the cross, you are a new creation, whether you feel like it or not. If tomorrow you wake up and you don't feel like a human, but you feel like a dog, it doesn't change the truth about who you are. No matter how powerful your canine feelings are, it's really weird for you to crawl around on all fours in your backyard and howl at the moon. It's not fitting because you are a person, not a dog. Christian, you may not feel like a new creation, especially since you're still in this old tent that is wearing out. But God says you are a new creation, in spite of your feelings. You can start living like a new creation. You are not bound to your old way of life.

Is there a way of living you need to reject—an old way—because you are a new creation? Jesus died for your sin. He died to reconcile you to God. Do you live out that reality? Or are you still living as if you're cut off from Him, as if your sin defines and controls you?

Ambassadors of Reconciliation

Because we are a new creation, we have a new homeland. We come from a new kingdom with new customs and new laws. Our allegiance is to our new King, and He has given us a special role to serve as His ambassadors in this world.

> Therefore, we are ambassadors for Christ, since God is making his appeal through us. We plead on Christ's behalf, "Be reconciled to God." (2 Cor. 5:20)

We are no longer natives here, so we cannot live and talk and love the same way as those who find this world to be their home. For us to be faithful ambassadors for Christ, we cannot be conformed to this world. Do you understand what we're saying? Part of our calling as ambassadors is to be distinct. We need to be distinct in the way we view people (we talked about this earlier). People have value, not for what they can do for us, but because they are made in the image of God. We don't misuse or abuse people, but serve them in love. Joining a church and assuming all the roles we've looked at—a worshipper of Jesus, a minister of the gospel, a servant of Jesus, a disciple-making disciple, a generous giver, and a faithful intercessor—will make us distinct. It will make us stand out as unique.

People will judge Jesus and His kingdom based upon their observations of us. Suppose you were chosen to serve as an ambassador to a people far away from here, a primitive people without access to the internet and television. In that case, all they know about your country is what they hear and see in you. They see you walk through the village center, and they say, "That's how Americans walk." They see you smile at a small child, and they assume, "Americans must all be kind to children." They see you get angry at your spouse and wonder, "Are all Americans selfish and short-tempered?" Everything they learn about America or Hungary or India comes from watching you.

People in your community know little to nothing about Jesus and His kingdom. How will they learn what Jesus is like? From watching you. You are a living advertisement for Jesus. You are a breathing billboard for the kingdom of heaven.

But maybe you think you're not qualified to be an ambassador. Surely there's some specialized training. No, the only prerequisite for serving as an ambassador is being reconciled to God through Jesus. That's the whole list. It's one thing long. Have you been reconciled to God? Yes? Great. You're hired! You are now an ambassador for Him. The power and ability to serve as ambassadors comes from His righteousness in us.[4]

As ambassadors we've been given "the ministry of reconciliation" (2 Cor. 5:18). This is our job, our calling. We are to bring the message of Christ's reconciliation with us everywhere we go.

Certainly your church does this each week when you gather in this embassy of heaven. You sing about Christ's work of reconciliation, you proclaim it from the Scriptures, and you celebrate it in the Lord's Supper. It's this weekly reminder that helps you go out into a foreign land ready to live and serve as ambassadors. You do this throughout the week with those around you who are still estranged from God. You tell them about Jesus, and you call them to be reconciled with God.

But the scope of our ministry is not limited to Sunday at church and individual conversations with non-Christians. We should seek to bring Christ's reconciliation anywhere we find strife and division. If there's a marriage that is struggling, we consider how to come alongside them as ministers of reconciliation. If a parent and child are in conflict, we think about how to help them reconcile. We notice the racial division in our community and carefully consider what part we can play in reconciliation. What about the division between rich and poor? Citizen and immigrant? Men and women? We ask how to bring reconciliation between those arguing about politics. Nothing is out of bounds. No area off-limits. As ministers of reconciliation, we seek to bring reconciliation anywhere we find conflict.

Of course, we cannot be faithful ambassadors bringing reconciliation if we can't get along ourselves. We've both experienced a wonderful spirit of unity in our churches. Unity that has lasted for years. Do we take it for granted? Certainly not. Are we eager to maintain the unity the Spirit of Christ has produced in us? Absolutely. But, this doesn't happen by chance. We have a responsibility for reconciliation. This won't happen if we're all easily offended or if we are unthinking and indifferent to other people's feelings. It won't happen if we're focused on our own comfort. It requires reaching out in personal ministry to others. It requires us to take our membership covenant seriously. We will care for one another in love. We will notice others, celebrating their blessings and weeping with them over their sorrows.

A ministry of reconciliation is not accomplished by paying a pastor to stand up front and preach about reconciliation. It's accomplished when members, like Bruce, enter conflict with kindness and humility, and are quick to forgive. When they realize no sin committed against them is worse than the sin they committed against God, and He still forgave them.

As ambassadors of Christ, we are ministers of reconciliation, and we've been given a message. An ambassador doesn't write his own material. He doesn't get to turn his preferences into policy. He's given the responsibility to speak on the king's behalf, so he's careful to only say what the king tells him to say. What is the message our king wants us to deliver? "Be reconciled to God" (2 Cor. 5:20). That's it. On behalf of Jesus, we plead with others to be reconciled to God.

This is a remarkable message. Usually the weak country without any hope for victory sends a message to the mighty king of the dominant nation pleading for leniency. Not the other way around. But Jesus, the offended and aggrieved party, pursues rebels and pleads with them to accept His mercy. Jesus doesn't plead because He is weak, and we are powerful. He pleads because His love is so great and our sin is so consuming. He pleads because He does not need us to validate Him. His love is so mighty, so powerful that He stoops low to rescue sinners.

The message of reconciliation is not long or elaborate. You don't have to memorize pages of text. You don't need a PhD to understand it. In English, it's just four words: "Be reconciled to God." And since we have been reconciled with God, we don't need to figure out clever ways to package this message. We just talk about what Jesus has done in us. We're like a flute, and the Spirit of God breathes in us, and out comes the music of reconciliation. All of this is from God. We're not left to do this work on our own.

> Working together with him, we also appeal to you, "Don't receive the grace of God in vain." For he says: At an acceptable time I listened to you, and in the day of salvation I helped you. See, now is the acceptable time; now is the day of salvation! (2 Cor. 6:1–2)

Our message is simple, but urgent. Paul calls those in the church, those receiving this letter, to make sure they aren't listening to the message and failing to respond. He warns them not to sit in church each week, hearing the truth, but not receiving it. It's possible to have God's grace presented to you, but to walk away empty-handed. He quotes from the prophet Isaiah to impress upon those listening that the time of salvation is right now.[5] Jesus has come! The day of salvation is here! Don't wait.

Don't put it on a list to do when you get older. Now is the time to respond to the message of reconciliation.

Every year, the National Weather Service chooses one week as "Severe Weather Preparedness Week." They create a plan to make sure we all know how to stay safe when severe weather strikes. They warn us using statistics: Lighting strikes the United States 25 million times and kills forty-seven people on average each year. They come up with mottos: "When Thunder Roars, Go Indoors" and "Turn Around, Don't Drown." They encourage us to make plans and prepare supplies. Meteorologists go on TV and keep us informed. All of it is done with one goal—to keep us safe.

In the same way, God has given each Christian a job to do. We're given an urgent message, and we're told to share it. As ambassadors of the gospel, this urgency cannot be lost on us. Carl F. H. Henry once said, "The gospel is only good news if it gets there in time."[6] We need to speak up. We don't need statistics or catchy slogans. We don't need gimmicks. Every Christian needs to proclaim and share the good news of Jesus Christ. We are ambassadors for Christ, and the way He warns and pleads with people is through us. Unlike a meteorologist, we're not warning our friends and neighbors about possible destruction sometime in the future, but a much bigger, much more urgent crisis right now. More than they need water and shelter, they need to be reconciled with God. It's our responsibility both individually and as a church to tell them. So we commit to speak up with greater boldness and to enter brokenness as ministers of reconciliation.

Conclusion

"You always know if someone goes to Harvard or if they go to CrossFit—they'll tell you."[7] This is the opening line of an article published in *The Atlantic* titled "The Church of CrossFit." The author of the article quotes a Harvard researcher who describes the passion of the CrossFit enthusiast as "evangelical zeal." Why do they have greater zeal for an exercise program than many Christians for sharing reconciliation with God? Could the reason be that Christians talk about sharing the gospel like the average person talks about going to the dentist? We often discuss the work of an ambassador like it's a necessary evil instead of an amazing invitation from Jesus to see lives transformed. How we talk about it matters. In our experience we've realized that most of the members of our churches already feel guilty for not sharing the gospel as faithfully as they should. Instead of doubling down on guilt, let's remind each other of the opportunity God is giving us. Let's help each other see what God is doing and how we have the privilege to take part.

We can talk about sharing the message of reconciliation with such enthusiasm that people will want to participate. Here's proof: One of the great college football coaches in the early years of the sport was Fielding Yost, coach of the University of Michigan for twenty-five years in the early 1900s. When he wanted to inspire his players, he used the language of evangelism to motivate them. Here's what he said:

> The Spirit of Michigan is based on a deathless loyalty to Michigan and all her ways, an enthusiasm that makes it second nature for Michigan Men to spread the gospel of their

> university to the world's distant outposts, and a conviction that nowhere is there a better university, in any way, than this Michigan of ours.[8]

Serving as an ambassador of Jesus Christ is so exciting a football coach stole the language to inspire his players. What could be more honorable and more worthwhile than giving your life to take the message of reconciliation with God to the world's distant outposts? If you are a Christian, the high court of heaven under the authority of the King of kings has commissioned you to serve as an officially designated "Ambassador of Reconciliation." What an honor. What a privilege. What a responsibility. What a way to spend your life.

Conclusion

The Swiss Army Knife exploded in popularity when American soldiers brought them home from Europe after World War II. The original Swiss Army Knife had wooden handles and a single blade which folded into the handle when not being used. What made it special was that it also included a reamer, can opener, and screwdriver. The can opener and reamer were intended to help soldiers open the metal cans which held their food rations, and the screwdriver made disassembling their service rifles much easier.[1] The second generation added a corkscrew and a smaller cutting blade.

If someone were to visit Switzerland and buy you an authentic Swiss Army Knife, you would expect more than a simple pocketknife with one blade. You would expect that one knife to include many other tools. If you take away all the other parts, it's just a knife, not a Swiss Army Knife. All those other tools are what make it unique and contribute to its identity and usefulness.

Attending church regularly is not what makes you a church member, just like having a single blade isn't what makes a knife a Swiss Army Knife. A biblically faithful church member is one title that includes many roles, and if you take away those roles, you lose what makes a church member unique and useful. A church member who doesn't worship, minister, serve, disciple, give, intercede, and evangelize is not living up to their name. But when a church member recognizes and embraces who Jesus Christ has called them to be, when you see the awesome opportunity and privilege God has given you to use your roles to serve Him, then you will discover how useful and effective a tool you can be in the hands of the divine carpenter.

We challenge you to embrace the awesome privilege of joining and serving in the church of Jesus Christ. Join a church for your good and His glory. Invest your life worshipping your King. Use your gifts to minister and serve His people. Steward your resources for the spread of His kingdom. Take the needs of your brothers and sisters before His throne. And invite rebels to receive mercy at His feet. There is no greater way to spend your life than in the service of Jesus and in the fellowship of His people.

Discussion Questions

Chapter One

1. What reasons might some people give for not joining a church?

2. Which reasons in this chapter for joining a church do you find most convincing?

3. If someone wasn't convinced church membership was in the Bible, what passage of Scripture would you show them?

4. Why don't people want accountability? Why is accountability so necessary?

5. How has involvement in a church been a help to your spiritual life?

6. In what ways would a lack of commitment negatively impact a person's ability to serve others in the church?

Chapter Two

1. How does our culture tempt us toward a worship experience tailored to our personal preferences?

2. What reasons do Christians need to worship with other Christians?

3. Christians, like sponges, soak up what's around them. What are you "soaking up" on a weekly basis?

4. One sign we're soaking up the Bible is that it shapes how we talk and think. List a couple examples you might point to in someone else's life as evidence that they are saturated with the Scriptures. Could others say that about you?

5. Why is singing together as a church important? How is it different from listening to worship music alone in your car?

6. Can you share a moment when God used a particular Sunday of worship in the church to encourage you?

Chapter Three

1. Why shouldn't we attempt to follow Jesus on our own?

2. In your opinion why has ministry in the church often been left to the pastors?

3. Evaluate your church involvement: Have you been active in ministry or more of a consumer?

4. Can you share an example of a church member who ministers to other members well? What makes their example stand out to you?

5. Why is it challenging to balance speaking truth and speaking in a loving way? Which is harder for you (truth or love)?

6. Read through the list of "one another's" (pp. 45–46). Choose a specific way you might obey it this week and spend time asking God to help you do that.

Chapter Four

1. Have you called on Jesus as your Lord? Share with someone how the Spirit led you from worshipping idols to following Jesus.

2. How has the Holy Spirit gifted you to serve other members of the body of Christ? Ask other Christians what gifts they see in you.

3. When are you most tempted to stay inside your bubble instead of serving people?

4. Has there been a time when you were tempted to make using your spiritual gifts more about self-fulfillment than meeting the needs of others?

5. Instead of asking yourself how you *want* to serve, consider asking someone at your church what needs you could meet with your gifts?

6. Make a short list of people in your church who are using their gifts to serve others. Spend some time thanking the Lord for each one of them.

Chapter Five

1. What does it mean to be a disciple? What did Jesus mean when He commanded us to make disciples?

2. What excuses do Christians often give for not making disciples?

3. Name an area of the Christian life in which you need to grow (like worshipping, serving, sharing the gospel, or praying). Who can you help grow in that same area?

4. People learn from our example. How can you invite someone to learn to follow Jesus from and with you?

5. Who has influenced your walk with Jesus? How did they influence you?

6. Picture a church where every member disciples another member. How would this church be different than other churches? What kind of impact could that make on your community?

Chapter Six

1. In what ways can generosity reveal good spiritual health?

2. Do you give sacrificially and regularly to your local church?

3. How have you seen churches love people well through their gifts?

4. Read Luke 12:13–34 and contrast a person who trusts his wealth to secure his future with a person who trusts God for future security.

5. What does your giving reveal about your understanding of God's grace?

6. How does stewarding and leveraging your financial resources help spread the gospel?

Chapter Seven

1. Why do you think so many Christians struggle to pray consistently?

2. What is one way you can discover how God is working in other members? How can you develop a pattern of thankfulness before God for these things?

3. How can prayer protect you from a critical spirit?

4. How does the promise of Philippians 1:6 encourage us to pray for others with confidence?

5. Is there another church member that is hard to love? Begin praying consistently for their spiritual growth and maturity.

6. How does prayer help you become less selfish?

Chapter Eight

1. Why do we need to be reconciled to God?

2. In what ways have you trespassed God's law?

3. How does the death of Jesus reconcile us with God?

4. Who are you most likely to criticize? How can the gospel help you when you are tempted to be critical?

5. Are there any previous sins that you continually allow to define you?

6. Your life is an advertisement for Jesus. When people watch you what do they think about Jesus?

7. Who can you come alongside as a minister of reconciliation?

Notes

Introduction

1. Ephesians 5:25; Hebrews 12:23

2. See Romans 1:7. Paul addresses all the Christians in Rome but also mentions a particular gathering in 16:5. See also 1 Corinthians 1:2 and Colossians 1:2.

Chapter One

1. 2 Timothy 2:3
2. 1 Timothy 6:12
3. 1 Peter 5:8
4. Acts 6:3
5. 1 Corinthians 5:1–5
6. Hebrews 3:13
7. Galatians 6:1
8. Throughout this book, we use the words *elder* and *pastor* to refer to the same office as described in 1 Timothy 3:1–7 and 1 Peter 5:1–5.
9. Elite Daily, "A Generation of Men Unwilling to Commit," *Huffington Post*, August 21, 2012, http://www.huffingtonpost.com/elite-daily/a-generation-of-men-unwilling_b_1812232.html.
10. Ephesians 2:19–22; 4:16

Chapter Two

1. Romans 12:1
2. 1 Corinthians 10:31
3. Acts 2:42–47

4. David A. Currie, *The Big Idea of Biblical Worship: The Development and Leadership of Expository Services* (Hendrickson, 2017), 18.

5. Colossians 1:7; 4:12

6. Colossians 4:16

7. J. I. Packer and Gary A. Parrett, *Grounded in the Gospel: Building Believers the Old-Fashioned Way* (Baker, 2010), 15.

8. Colossians 3:5–11

9. Colossians 3:12–17

10 Colossians 3:13

11. C. S. Lewis, *Mere Christianity* (Collier, 1960), 104.

12. Colossians 3:14–15

13. Dietrich Bonhoeffer, *Life Together: The Classic Exploration of Christian in Community* (HarperOne, 2009), 20.

14. Edward Mote, "My Hope Is Built on Nothing Less," public domain.

Chapter Three

1. Charles Austin Miles, "In the Garden," public domain.

2. 1 Corinthians 15:58

3. Matthew 20:28

4. Ephesians 4:7

5. Tim Chester, *You Can Change: God's Transforming Power for Our Sinful Behavior and Negative Emotions* (Crossway, 2010), 158.

6. Romans 8:29

7. Ephesians 4:11–16

8. Romans 8:13

9. John 13:35

Chapter Four

1. 1 Corinthians 2:12; 3:16; 6:19

2. D. A. Carson, *Showing the Spirit: A Theological Exposition of 1 Corinthians 12–14* (Baker, 1987), 32.

3. 1 Corinthians 12:28. We find even more gifts in Romans 12:6–8.

4. Warren Wiersbe, *Be Wise (1 Corinthians): Discern the Difference Between Man's Knowledge and God's Wisdom* (David C. Cook, 2010), 137.

Chapter Five

1. 1 Thessalonians 2:7
2. 1 Corinthians 11:1; Philippians 3:17; 1 Thessalonians 1:6–7; 2 Thessalonians 3:7–9
3. 2 Timothy 4:6–7
4. 1 Timothy 4:12
5. Titus 2:3–5

Chapter Six

1. Luke 21:1–4
2. Acts 5
3. 3 John 5
4. Acts 2:45
5. 1 Corinthians 16:1–2
6. Philippines 4:15
7. 1 Timothy 5:17–18
8. 3 John 6, 9–10
9. 3 John 9
10. 3 John 10
11. 3 John 8
12. Karen H. Jobes, *1, 2, & 3 John*, Exegetical Commentary on the New Testament (Zondervan Academic, 2014), 306.
13. 1 Chronicles 29:13
14. Lee Strobel, "What a Poor Chicago Family Taught Me One Christmas Eve," *Investigating Faith with Lee Strobel* email newsletter, November 10, 2018.
15. Strobel, "What a Poor Chicago Family Taught Me."

Chapter Seven

1. Ephesians 1:1, 15
2. Ephesians 1:7

3. Tony Merida and Francis Chan, *Exalting Jesus in Philippians*, Christ-Centered Exposition (B&H, 2016), 22.

4. Philippians 1:8

5. Philippians 1:7

6. Philippians 1:9

7. Philippians 1:10

8. Philippians 1:10–11

Chapter Eight

1. 2 Corinthians 5:21

2. John Piper, "We Exult in God Through Our Lord Jesus Christ," December 19, 1999, https://www.desiringgod.org/messages/we-exult-in-god-through-our-lord-jesus-christ.

3. 2 Corinthians 6:1

4. 2 Corinthians 5:21

5. Isaiah 49:8

6. This quotation is commonly attributed to Carl F. H. Henry.

7. Julie Beck, "The Church of CrossFit," *The Atlantic*, June 24, 2017, https://www.theatlantic.com/health/archive/2017/06/the-church-of-crossfit/531501/.

8. John U. Bacon, *Endzone: The Rise, Fall, and Return of Michigan Football* (St. Martin's Griffin, 2015), 424.

Conclusion

1. "The Story Behind the Swiss Army Knife," Alpenwild, https://www.alpenwild.com/staticpage/swiss-army-knife-history-and-facts/, accessed on June 10, 2024.

About the Authors

Josh Wredberg serves as lead pastor of Redeemer Community Church in Fuquay-Varina, North Carolina. He has earned a doctorate in preaching from Southeastern Baptist Theological Seminary. Josh is the coauthor of *Exalting Jesus in John*—a commentary in the Christ-Centered Exposition series. He is the founder and president of Christ-Centered & Clear, a ministry that helps pastors become better preachers. He and his wife, Cari, have three sons, Jack, Max, and Caed.

Matthew Z. Capps has served as the lead pastor of Fairview Baptist Church in Apex, North Carolina, since 2015. Capps is a graduate of Southeastern Baptist Theological Seminary (MDiv in Biblical Languages), Gordon-Conwell Theological Seminary (DMin in Pastoral Theology), and is a PhD candidate at Ridley College in Melbourne, Australia. Capps is the author of *Hebrews: A 12-Week Study* (Crossway, 2015), contributor to *15 Things Seminary Couldn't Teach Me* (Crossway, 2018), editor of *The Timeless Truths Bible* (Thomas Nelson, 2023), author of *Drawn by Beauty* (B&H Academic, 2025), *Every Member Matters* (B&H, 2025), and *A Short Guide to Church Revitalization* (B&H, 2026). Matt and Laura have three children: Solomon, Ruby, and Abby.